"With grace and humility, Jenn reaches out to tell other abuse survivors that there is hope and a future beyond their pain. Giving advice grounded in Scripture, Jenn walks through her personal process of healing with lived-it advice for others on the same path. If you have been abused or are supporting a loved one who has experienced abuse, you will find solace and wisdom here."

KARLA JACOBS, Member, Georgia Commission on Women, Georgia Human Trafficking Task Force

"Gripping, grievous, gracious, glorious, and gut-wrenching. Greenberg sets straight the path."

LORI ANNE THOMPSON, Survivor and Storyteller

"In *Not Forsaken*, if you have experienced abuse, you will feel understood. If you have not, you will understand better the impact that abuse has. Statistics show abuse is rampant in our world and Christian communities. This is a reminder of how much we must do to protect the innocent, and of how there is hope in Jesus for those who suffer."

DR. TIMOTHY S. LANE, President, Institute for Pastoral Care; Author, *How People Change* and *Unstuck*

"Starting a domestic-abuse ministry has been a long road with a steep learning curve. This is the book I wish we would have had at the beginning."

JASON MEYER, Pastor for Preaching and Vision, Bethlehem Baptist Church, Minneapolis

"A powerful and needed book, as the prevalence of abuse increasingly comes to light in our world and churches. This book will not only be a healing balm for the deepest wounds but will leave you worshiping the God of hope, healing, and redemption."

SARAH WALTON, Author, *Hope When It Hurts*

"Jennifer is exactly the kind of expert that nobody wants to be: she has firsthand experience of the destructive nature of abuse. In spite of this she gives a firsthand account of the power of love. This book combines the compassion of #metoo experience with the wisdom of a seasoned theologian."

BOB HAMP, Marriage and Family Therapist; Author, *Think Differently* series

"A brave and authentic exploration of the complex and often conflicting feelings and actions that accompany abuse. The shared human condition of pain shines through this book, but in a way that brings you hope, healing, and a future beyond that pain."

NICOLE F. FISHER, President, Health & Human Rights Strategies

"For those who want a faith-based process of healing, this lays the foundation to take the first step to wholeness."

TODD HILDEBRANDT, Survivor; RAINN Speakers Bureau

"Jennifer's book offers God's powerful truths through the aching realities of her own testimony. She gives you permission to feel, heal, and discover who you are through the murky waters of the abuse that has tried to drown you. I am grateful for Jennifer's voice and her bravery: everyone will benefit from reading *Not Forsaken*!"

POLLY HAMP, Survivor; Author, *Cherished*

"If you want to see how the gospel meets those who have been hurt and abused, pick up this powerful book. And if you lead in any capacity in the church, have several copies on hand to help give hope to those who feel hopeless."

DANIEL DARLING, VP for Communications, The Ethics and Religious Liberty Commission; Author, *The Dignity Revolution*

"Few books truly have the power to change a person's life, but I believe this is one of them. *Not Forsaken* is one of the most powerful, chilling, heartbreaking, redemptive, and inspiring stories I've ever read. Jenn invites the reader to join her on a journey from heartbreak to healing; and along the way, you'll experience the full range of human emotion and see the goodness of God in new ways."

DAVE WILLIS, Author, *Raising Boys Who Respect Girls*

"Deeply moving. As a survivor, each chapter spoke to my personal experiences and felt validating and fulfilling. Jenn brings her spirituality and compassion to her work and to those who benefit from her kindness and her story. I count myself as one of them."

CHAD FELIX GREENE, Survivor, Advocate and Author

"Jenn doesn't shy away from the awful and ugly experiences she has endured; but she also paints a beautiful picture of redemption. As an abuse survivor, Jenn's words resonated with me. For spouses, family members, or friends seeking to understand abuse in a loved one, this book is perfect. For pastors, teachers, and leaders, this book will be a resource you will find yourself pulling off your bookshelf again and again as you walk beside survivors in your church, ministry, or school."

MEGAN LIVELY, Survivor; Founder, Relevant Reach

"If you've never experienced abuse, take a moment to thank God. Then read this book to enter the scary world populated, perhaps, by your friends, family, church members, and neighbors. The church needs this message."

WILLIAM BOEKESTEIN, Pastor, Immanuel Fellowship Church, Kalamazoo, Michigan; Author, *The Future of Everything*

"This is the riveting story of a young woman finding redemption from abuse by family and church. While not easy reading, it will help the church learn anew how to defend the weak and mistreated. Pastors and church leaders are urged to read *Not Forsaken*."

BARRY YORK, President and Professor of Pastoral Theology, Reformed Presbyterian Theological Seminary

"What is one of the most beneficial forms of care we can provide for those who have been abused? Listening. Does that make you uncomfortable? It's better to admit it and grow than ignore the awkwardness. Jenn Michelle Greenberg has given us an opportunity to listen, which will help us do better when someone we know shares their story with us. Allow her vulnerability and courage to equip you for when someone entrusts you to pastor or befriend them as they navigate the aftershocks of abuse."

J.D. GREEAR, President, The Southern Baptist Convention

"I recommend this work to everyone, as a glorious reminder that we are not forsaken. In a culture saturated with victimhood and self-reflection, Jennifer takes us to the transcendent God who alone gives hope in the struggle of life through Jesus Christ."

PROF. DUSTIN BENGE, The Andrew Fuller Center for Baptist Studies

"The church has been crying out for a book like this, and the right person has now written it in the right way. Yes, it's raw, honest, transparent, and painful. That's why it will resonate with so many. But, unlike so many secular abuse memoirs, this one is also full of grace, truth, gospel, and hope. That's why it will be redemptive for so many."

DR. DAVID MURRAY, Professor of Old Testament and Practical Theology, Puritan Reformed Seminary

"*Not Forsaken* offers a glimpse into the heart and mind of an abuse survivor, both during and after the abuse. With skillful compassion, Jenn offers hope from the story of the gospel. A helpful and hope-giving guide for abuse survivors and caregivers alike."

ERIC SCHUMACHER, Co-author,
Worthy: Celebrating the Value of Women

JENNIFER MICHELLE
GREENBERG

NOT

———

FORSAKEN

A STORY OF LIFE
AFTER ABUSE

Not Forsaken: A Story of Life After Abuse
© Jennifer Michelle Greenberg, 2019

Published by:
The Good Book Company

thegoodbook.com | www.thegoodbook.co.uk
thegoodbook.com.au | thegoodbook.co.nz | thegoodbook.co.in

This book recounts events in the life of the author according to the author's recollection and from the author's perspective. Dialogue, names, dates, places, events, and details may be been altered for privacy purposes or literary effect.

Hardcover ISBN: 9781784984380 | Paperback ISBN: 9781784984526

Printed in India

Design by André Parker

CONTENTS

FOREWORD
by Russell Moore

"I have found, in short, from reading my own writing, that my subject in fiction is the action of grace in territory held largely by the devil," novelist Flannery O'Connor once wrote. I reflect on that insight often, because I think it applies much more broadly than to the realm of literature. What is most real in the cosmos is just that: the action of grace in territory held largely by the devil.

As Christians, we see both the horror of evil and, against that, the triumphant beauty of the gospel of Jesus Christ. We don't see the world, or history, or our own life plotlines as sentimental morality tales, nor do we see them as gothic horror stories. As we follow Jesus, we see the world around us through the prism of the cross. And at the cross we see the nauseating brokenness of this devil-haunted universe, and, even more than that, the grace of one who poured out his own blood to save us.

Christians, then, should be, above all people, those who understand the reality of trauma. And we should be, above all people, those who know that trauma is not invincible to the workings of grace. We see human lives, including our own, in terms of the Place of the Skull—a sight that causes broken hearts to turn away in grief and a sight that causes broken hearts to shout for joy at the truth that while the valley of the shadow of death is real indeed, there is a Shepherd there alongside us.

This book is a word of testimony from one who has lived through trauma, and is able, as the Bible tells us, to groan at the wreckage of a satanized world and to cry out, by the Spirit, "Abba, Father" (Romans 8 v 12-17). As you read these moving reflections, you may find that you are being helped to deal with events in your own past or present, by seeing them in the light of the gospel of hope. And if, like me, you have not faced such evil yourself, you might stop to wonder what awful realities are around you right now from which you might be turning your head in apathy.

My prayer is that all of us might wonder what are the ways—ways very different from one life to the next—in which the grace of God has moved people, or can move them, from "victim" to "survivor." Those questions might prompt us to stand up for justice for those who are being harmed. And they might propel us to remember what many of us learned to sing, before we really understood just how painful it can be to live:

Grace has brought me safe thus far,
And grace will lead me home.

Russell Moore
President, The Ethics and Religious Liberty Commission

"Never will I leave you;
never will I forsake you."

Hebrews 13 v 5b

5

She patted the dirt firmly into the pot. This would be a perfect addition to her caterpillar farm. The brick patio was littered with spare pots and bags of soil. Not quite in kindergarten, she loved spending her days outside, digging through earth, planting weeds, and collecting bugs.

"I can't read very good," she explained to God as she tilled soil with her fingers. "The Bible is too long and praying with my eyes closed is boring. How about, when I talk in my head, I'll be talking to you?"

She remembered her mother reading the Bible and telling her about the wisdom of King Solomon. He had asked for wisdom from God, and God had lavished it upon him. More than anything she wanted to be smart like her daddy: the spiritually aware man of science, the researcher, reader, and authority on doctrine and evolution. She prayed that God would make her wise like Solomon. Most of all, she prayed that God would allow her to see demons, just like Jesus had, so she could know good people from evil.

10

"Be quiet," he said. "I am reading."

Her father once again addressed himself to the thick theology book with its elegant hardcover and advanced Biblical theorem. The little girl nodded agreement and went back to playing, this time keeping her voice down. Suddenly, a strong hand grabbed her from behind. He clenched her arm tightly, shook her violently, and began to beat her.

She cried out that she was sorry. She promised to be quiet. She screamed for help. He would not stop hitting. In an instant, her father had gone from studying apologetics to beating his daughter.

At the sounds of her screams, her mother ran into the room.

"What are you doing?" she demanded.

Her father dropped her, and she fled into her room. There, huddled on the floor, she examined the hand-shaped welts. She lined her small fingers up with each bruise: five purple contusions for each place his fingers had gripped her.

"This is how big my dad's hands are," she thought.

In the living room, her father went back to reading his theology book.

12

She jolted awake to her heart racing, her skin crawling in a cold sweat, and her stomach writhing with anxiety. She looked at the clock.

2:00 am.

It was that same horrible dream. As so many times before, the demon had thrown open her bedroom door, leapt onto her bed, and ripped off the covers. Somehow, she knew, the demon represented her dad.

"It's only a dream," she told herself. "Only a dream."

But she was terrified.

She had seen his porn. It seemed that almost every night he planted more of it on her computer, and every day she found grotesque new images. There were rape scenes, torture scenes, scenes of multiple men raping a teen girl. Sometimes she'd catch him watching her as she logged into her desktop, staring at her with that cold brightness in his eyes.

Day after day brought more shame and fear. Night after night brought recurring nightmares.

She began to lock her bedroom door.

She tied bells around the doorknob and left obstacles, like shoes, toys, and a box of knick-knacks, on the path to her bed. *If he comes in while I'm sleeping,* she thought, *he'll trip and the noise will wake me up.*

"God," she prayed one night, weeping alone in the dark, "this man I live with is not my dad. He's a stranger. I don't know if I can grow up like this. I need You to be my Daddy.

Please God, fill that role in my life. I know you can't be here physically, and I need someone who is here, but don't leave me alone as an orphan."

And God answered.

It was as if love were an ocean, and she had been plunged into the very heart of it. Her fear was washed away, and her sorrow dispersed like fog on a summer morning. Without a shadow and without exception, she knew she was God's daughter, and she laughed through her tears at that swift relief.

15

She held the razor blade against her arm.

She knew what she had to do.

She knew how to do it.

She remembered the time when she was about four years old, sitting at the dinner table with her dad. It was an oval walnut table she'd always thought was fancy. Her mom was cleaning up dishes, and she was sitting in the chair nearest the kitchen. He was sitting at the head of the table, to her left.

He was talking about a man who had tried to commit suicide. She didn't remember if it was a story he'd seen on the news or heard about at work. It didn't really matter. He was a loser, her dad said, and there's no bigger loser than someone who can't even kill themselves.

Then he looked at her, and he taught her how to kill herself. He explained how to cut in such a way that, if EMTs found her before she bled out, they'd find it almost impossible to save her. He showed her the vein on his arm as he spoke and had her show him the vein on her arm.

Her mom hissed and gave him a reprimanding look. The girl never forgot that night at the dinner table. She never forgot thinking, "Daddy wants me to kill myself."

For decades her memory of his words would echo in her mind.

For years she tried to rationalize them.

Maybe it was for her good. Maybe her dad knew sometimes life gets really hard. Maybe sometimes you need a way out. Maybe all good parents prepare their kids to escape awful lives, should the need arise.

Those chilling words seared into her memory.

It will be almost impossible to save you.

Fast-forward about a decade. She was 15, sitting on her wrought iron twin-sized bed, white and gold with roses. She loved that bed. She remembered her mom waking her up on her birthday morning when she was about seven by spreading a new white comforter over her. It was all so pretty in the sunlight: the painted iron flowers, the curve of the headboard, the sparkly gold knobs.

She held the razor blade against her arm.

She knew what to do. Her dad had taught her well.

His terrible words, like seeds planted deep, had taken root in her mind and sprouted poisonous vines.

She'd recently overheard her dad telling her mom what a gorgeous figure she was developing. It hadn't sounded fatherly. It had sounded like a sexual compliment from the same man who was planting images of middle-aged men having sex with teenagers on her computer. She felt the walls closing in on her.

"Clearly," she thought, "I'm some kind of pervert: some kind of disease. I may not sin myself, but I infect other people with sin. Dad doesn't love me. Why doesn't he love me? Or is this all in my head? Am I a pervert for imagining my dad is attracted to me, yet hates me? Why would someone be attracted to someone they hate? That doesn't make sense. Maybe I'm losing my mind. Or maybe dad stays emotionally distant and gets angry because he's trying not to be tempted by me. Maybe he's being valiant by avoiding me. Maybe his coldness is self-sacrificing. Maybe I'm the problem."

Her mom often fussed at her to wear "modest" clothes: jean shorts that went down to her knees, turtle necks, and high-necked sleeved shirts. Some of it was normal mom stuff. However, it reinforced the girl's fear that she was causing her dad to grow evil.

Drowning in confusion and fear, she reached out and grasped at God.

She held the razor to her skin as she wept and prayed.

"God, I want to die, but I'm scared. I've heard that people who commit suicide go to hell. I don't want to go to hell. God, please forgive me. Please, give me a sign so I know you'll take me to heaven."

There are very few moments in life when God tears through the darkness like a lightning bolt. But at that moment, he did. Everything turned bright white. She looked down and saw her bedroom below. It was as if she were suspended, hovering over her bed. Everything was soundless like a silent film. She saw her mom throw open the door and rush to her lifeless body. Her two little sisters huddled frightened in the doorway.

Then a voice broke the silence.

"I will never leave you or forsake you."

It was an ancient voice, but an ageless voice. It was full of profound strength, yet as gentle as a loving daddy toward his newborn baby. Though she'd never heard that voice before, she instinctively knew it was God. It was as if recognition of his voice was woven into the fabric of her DNA.

And suddenly, as if someone had flicked off the lights, she was sitting on her bed again, holding a razor blade against her arm, crying in the dark.

She dropped it.

She knew.

She had a Father in heaven who loved her. He would never betray her or abandon her. No matter what she did, no matter what her biological father did, God would always be her Daddy.

And what would her suicide do to her mother and sisters? Despite her fear and agony, she knew her death would cause more pain than her life. She decided to be brave. She retrieved the razor from the floor and hid it in her dresser, just in case she ever changed her mind. After all, you never know how bad life might get, do you? Her dad had prepared her for that.

Then she stayed in her room. She waited to see how long it would have taken for them to find her body.

But they never came.

No one ever came.

She waited several hours.

"I'd definitely have bled out by now," she thought. "I would not have been a failure."

And she went downstairs to find something to eat.

15

It was going to be a wonderful weekend. She was on her way to church summer camp, away from her dad, chores, nightmares, homework, and stress. She would make friends, relax, go swimming, and maybe even meet some nice boys.

Oh yes. She was looking forward to this.

The drive to camp was a good ten hours. To break up the journey, she and the friends she was carpooling with would stay overnight at a pastor's house. You could see for miles around his country home. She enjoyed chicken fights, the pool, dinner on the patio, and finally curling up in bed unconcerned about who might be watching her. Around midnight she got up for a glass of water.

There he was, sitting on the sofa.

As a pastor, he explained, he was often up late writing sermons or planning church functions. He was glad she was up though, because he wanted to talk to her about something.

"When you were in the pool," he said, "I noticed you acting very sexually. The sensuality oozed from you."

She felt her face flush. Was he picking up on things that were happening with her dad? Was her contamination so obvious? Her relaxing evening free of accusation and innuendo vaporized in a puff of humiliation.

"You've got to understand," the pastor continued, "boys your age are just beginning to discover their sexuality. As a female, you're miles ahead of them. They're starting to understand body language and notice things like hips and cleavage. When you tread water in the pool—your breasts protruding under your swimsuit, your figure out there for everyone to see—it catches their attention. You make them think about sex."

She began strategizing ways to end this horrible conversation. She mumbled that she hadn't meant to do anything inappropriate. She'd simply been having fun with friends. She considered telling him that her dad had picked out her swimsuit himself, but then she felt a pang of fear, and stayed quiet.

That's too complicated, she thought.

"I don't want you to feel embarrassed or on the spot," the pastor chattered on. "This is a conversation I've had with my daughters, because I want them to be ready for the real world and aware of their vulnerabilities. If you know what your vulnerabilities are, you can protect yourself. Make sense? So, let me ask you, what would it take to get you to spread your legs for a man?"

She was dumbfounded. No one, not even dad, had ever asked her such a question.

"I don't feel comfortable with this conversation," she said.

He prattled on, but she managed to excuse herself. Once she was safely back in bed, she realized she'd forgotten her water, and cried herself to sleep.

A few weeks later, when she was back at home, she told her parents what the pastor had said. They invited him over for dinner. They had her sing the pastor a song. They never told anyone what had happened.

─────────── 17 ───────────

Broken glass sprayed the back of her legs. She looked down expecting to see blood, but there was none. Her mom had gone to the grocery store, leaving her to make her dad lunch, and he was not happy about how long it was taking.

She said nothing. Speaking might enrage him even more.

He smashed another plate down behind her, tearing a chunk out of the linoleum flooring. Fragments of glass tinkled across the kitchen, bouncing off cabinets, chair legs, and walls.

She remained silent, her body trembling with a fear that was quickly transforming into rage.

She felt a fork whiz past her head, hit the cabinets, and clatter to the floor. A knife flew next, making her heart jump, leaving a dent in the woodwork inches from her face.

She couldn't take it any longer. She was his daughter, she thought. If he could be terrifying, so could she. She turned around and faced him.

"I am not afraid of you!" she screamed. "Sit down and be quiet or I will call the police."

She felt his rage diminish slightly. She thought he almost looked impressed, but that expression was quickly replaced by what she thought might be resentment. He sat down at the table. She finished making his lunch.

18

"Marry a rich man," he told her. There was, he said, no practical reason for women to have educations. A college degree was just an expensive political statement. Women don't really want careers or to earn money. Don't be stupid, was the message: "marry a rich man."

But he couldn't stop her. College was her escape route, her trap door, her only hope. She was going.

Having been accepted into a prestigious opera school, she lived at home but took a bus to campus. After a few weeks, she met a boy. He was a quiet mechanical engineering major who never got angry. He gave her food when she was hungry. He listened to her read the Bible to him. He made her feel cared about. He gave her a purpose.

But her dad seemed to sense an independent spirit growing inside her: hints of hope and a fixation on the future.

"Men only think of you as a piece of meat," he said. "This one is no different."

Her scholarships ran out. Her dad wouldn't help with funding. Staying in college became seemingly impossible. In tears, she dropped out.

Two years later, the young man asked her dad if he could marry her. He had his degree now, a job, and plans to buy a house.

"No," her dad said.

That night she asked her mom, "What do we do now?"

"Get married," her mom said. "Elope if you have to. Get away from your dad. He's a bad man."

So, she and the boy defied her father.

The young man proposed. She planned a wedding. He took her to tour model homes. Let her pick out carpet. Paint colors.

When her dad threatened her, she made sure to take his gun and hide it.

They went to Colorado for their honeymoon. And the more she got to know her husband, the more she realized what kind of man her dad was.

It was all so strange and new.

But she was free.

—————— 21 ——————

S he sat in the pews, alone in the crowd. It felt more like a morgue than a church to her. This was the sanctuary where her dad had once worshiped. These were the seats where her family had sat mutely. And now the truth was beginning to come out, and she could feel the glances on the back of her neck—sense the sorrowful and shocked whispers. She'd never imagined how embarrassing being believed could be.

Dead memories. Unseeing eyes. She needed air. Whispering an excuse to her husband, she left the sanctuary to roam quiet halls. She tried to breathe deep and walk off her jitters. After a while, she paused to stare at a painting on the wall.

The colors begin to swim.

She didn't hear him approach. The man said her name. He sounded like her dad. It wasn't his fault, of course. But the sudden adrenaline rush plunged her into a panic attack.

She couldn't breathe. She doubled over, gasping. After overcoming his surprise, the man ran to get her husband. It was as if the wind had been knocked out of her, except every time she thought the pressure couldn't get worse, it did. She felt like her lungs were going to burst. Her heart pounded in her head like a drum.

Why hadn't she passed out yet? In the movies, when someone is oxygen-deprived or in severe pain, they faint. In real life, you keep agonizing in acute awareness until you think you might die.

Finally, her husband arrived. He grabbed her, picked her up, and held her tight until she calmed down. Once the adrenaline wore off, she felt exhausted as if drugged. It was a zoned-out state, a terrifying state, as if she was only partially awake.

Once church let out, everyone saw her. Tear-streaked cheeks, vacant expression, husband crying. She would always regret that: she had made her newly-wed husband cry. She knew it wasn't her fault, but she felt she should be stronger. He shouldn't have to pay for what her dad had done.

"You should find a new church," a therapist later advised.

It was true.

There were too many memories haunting that place.

Too much history between those four walls.

22

The first year of marriage was a dream. She had finally escaped. She felt loved and free, and it was exhilarating. But then understanding crept in, and with it came questions. She struggled to trust her husband's strange, patient ways. More than once she'd fought with him, paranoid that his love was false—a thing too good to be true.

One night she saw him: her husband, washing dishes.

"You forgot to do the dishes?" a voice in her head said. "You're a pathetic wife. He's going to leave you. I'd give him two years, max. He's a patient guy, but you're worthless. You'll be alone. Abandoned."

Cue panic.

"What are you doing?" she demanded.

"The dishes," he replied, looking confused.

"Great! Now he's suspicious of you," the voice hissed. "Don't show him how crazy you are. Stay calm! You've got to hide it. Control it! You're an awful wife. You can't keep the house clean, and when he tries to help with chores, you act ridiculous. Maybe you're not cut out for marriage. Maybe he's better off without you."

She didn't want to seem too upset, otherwise he might realize she was nuts. But her breathing grew jagged and the urge to cry increased. She begged him to stop and insisted she could be a good wife. She demanded he put the sponge down and step away from the sink. Her husband, for his part, stubbornly kept washing dishes.

As she gave up and walked away, the voice laughed at her.

"You're stupid, hyper-emotional, and can't even keep the house clean," it said. "You're just a piece of meat. Sex is the only reason he'll ever stay with you."

Those words ripped open a wound she thought had healed. The bitterness was shocking, but the poison familiar. Suddenly she was a teenager again in her father's house, and he was lecturing her on the perfidious ways of men.

That's when she realized, to her horror, that the voice in her head sounded just like her dad.

23

Over the past years, her dad's control over himself and his family had crumbled. The lack of incentive to lie unleashed more of the violence and dysfunctionality he'd previously restrained. Familial relationships devolved into distrust, bitterness, and heartbreak. Foolish pastors gave poor advice, wise pastors gave unheeded advice, and sins once committed in secret were now openly flaunted. He still wanted them to pretend they were happy, but they would not. Not anymore.

As she and her husband were driving home from a date, the cell phone rang. It was her little sister's birthday, so a call from her mother wasn't unexpected—but what she said was.

"Your dad was angry because your sister didn't want to go out with him," her mother wept. "He smashed a drinking glass on the table so hard there's glass stuck in the wood. He used the broken glass to stab himself in the arm while he screamed, 'This is how much I love you! This is how much I love you!' There's blood everywhere."

The police were called.

They told him to leave.

They told him to get help.

He never came home again.

30

She looked into her child's eyes.

"I need you, Mommy," the little girl said affectionately, twirling her mother's hair around tiny fingers.

All those years of childhood, and for over a decade after, she'd tried to fix broken people she loved. She'd played the part of the good daughter, hoping her dad would love her. She'd fought with him, pleaded, and challenged him to be a good man, until it became clear that he was who he wanted to be, and her husband told her dad to never speak to her again.

And now here she was. A parent herself. A mom, with a little three-year-old daughter who needed her, and trusted her, and who felt safe and secure.

There was no more need to fix. No more need to search for love and approval. No more need to agonize over *Why?* Somehow along the way, she realized she'd always had a heavenly Father. He had brought her through. He had always loved her. And with his help, her little girl would know a very different home than she had. And with his help, her little girl would learn of the Father who would never forsake her, no matter how dark or desperate this world became.

I am that mom.

I was that girl.

1. THIS IS
MY STORY

I will never tell you that if God loves you, you'll have a dramatic spiritual experience. I've only had a few, and each occurred during life-or-death situations. Some will say I hallucinated when I heard God's voice. Maybe I did. Some will think I imagined it because it's what my mind knew I needed to hear in order to survive. However, I've prayed many times. I've wept for hours and begged for signs. I've yearned for a supernatural jolt to rekindle weak faith. Usually, there is silence in return.

God has only stabbed through the spiritual veil for me a few times, and only when I'd have made a horrendous mistake if he hadn't. Other times, when I was terrified and depressed, and longed wholeheartedly for a sign, I didn't get one. But when I did, the fact that the words spoken were straight from the Bible assures me of their authenticity, hallucination or no.

Maybe I did hallucinate. If an event occurs in your mind, does that mean it never really happened? Does it mean it isn't important? Of course not! Many things happen only in our minds, and yet have profound impacts on our lives and the lives of others. Logical thought, joy, sorrow, ambition, inner conflict, faith—all these things are valid, real, and important, yet only exist in our heads. God works through means. If God chose to use a hallucination to save my life, I'm okay with that.

You don't need to have a dramatic experience to be saved or to know that God loves you. Faith is not based on the flashiness of your testimony, and God doesn't work the same way in everyone's life. Your experiences may be totally unlike mine. Nevertheless, we are created in the image of the same God. As such, we share many emotions and the way we experience pain is often the same.

I have a friend who was badly beaten as a boy. Though we're completely different people on the outside (I'm a young mom, and he's a middle-aged divorcee), we've suffered the same depression, told ourselves the same lies, and experienced the same confusion on the inside. Little of the abuse we endured was the same. Our upbringing was different and our parents dissimilar. However, the psychological and emotional effects—the post-traumatic spiritual injuries—are nearly identical. I've found this to be true with virtually every abuse survivor I've encountered, and even some veterans with PTSD.

How can this be?

I theorize that, regardless of the type of weapon used against us, the injury inflicted is comparable. If I get shot in the shoulder and you get stabbed in the shoulder, we both have lacerated shoulders. Generally speaking, we'll need very similar surgery, stitches, painkillers, and physical therapy. Just so, emotional injuries sustained through different means often exhibit similar damage.

If you have suffered abuse, then, as members of a tragically large club no one wants to join, we share a pain that is strikingly consistent. We've drunk the same poison from different cups. You've just read some of what I experienced—and there are other events from my childhood that have not been detailed in these pages. Many of you who read this book will have suffered far worse than me. Some may feel too damaged to ever feel joy again. Others may think their abuse was "no big deal," yet dream of a day when they feel whole again. Whatever your background, wherever you are in the recovery process, your suffering is unjust, real, and important. No level of abuse is too minor to matter, and no survivor is too broken to feel God's healing grace. I'm so glad you're reading. Thank you.

Or maybe you were never abused, but desire to understand and help someone who was. You should know that this book began as a personal letter to Jason, my husband, to help him understand me, and to tell him many things that I didn't know how to say. Hopefully, what I have told him will also empower you. And I'm so grateful to you for taking the time to understand my journey. I want you to know that whoever you're helping is blessed to have you in their lives.

Isn't it tragic that in a world so beautiful and diverse, a defining feature we all have in common is pain? While I'd never wish our suffering on anyone, there are benefits to this sameness. We can take comfort knowing that despite how we feel, we aren't isolated oddities. Though our injuries were inflicted under different circumstances by different abusers using different weapons, our wounds are consistent. Thus, the same balm can heal us all.

This book is about that balm. It's about the journey I traveled through the Valley of the Shadow of Death; the things that guided me; the milestones which helped me process my trauma and recover. It's still raw, of course. We may always bear scars this side of heaven. You'll see some of mine in this book. But ultimately, this is a story about hope, about healing, and about a future beyond our pain. The Bible calls

Jesus a Wonderful Counselor and a Great Physician. Let me tell you how he healed me.

> *I would rather walk with a friend in the*
> *dark, than alone in the light. (Helen Keller)*

2. WAS I ABUSED?

*She did the worst thing to me that anyone
can do to anyone else. Let them believe that
they're loved and wanted and then show them
that it's all a sham.*

(Agatha Christie, *The Mirror
Crack'd from Side to Side*)

Did my dad abuse me? I wasn't even sure. Some family
friends were furious and called him a monster. Others
seemed to think I was lying or mentally unstable. I began
to question everything, including my own perception. My
understanding of fatherhood, marriage, and masculinity was
wrong. My understanding of love, family, and morality was
bent. And I considered that if I'd been so deceived before,
who was I to say I wasn't deceived now? I was disoriented.
Overwhelmed.

I remember the first book I ever read on "how to recover from abuse." My plan was to compare my experiences to
stories in the book and see where my abuse fell on the scale
between "minor" and "severe." I hoped I'd feel better if I
could say, "My abuse wasn't all that bad; therefore I'm not a
victim." I thought minimizing my experiences would minimize my pain.

I was wrong.

Poring over extreme cases of abuse, trying to make myself
feel better by pretending my abuse was inconsequential,

backfired. It made me feel stupid and even crazy. There were horrifying crimes depicted on those pages, many completely different from my own experiences. I started to wonder if my trauma was unjustified: if I should be able to suck it up, but was too weak to do so.

I even questioned whether I'd really been abused. One pastor told me, "Unless he hit you with a closed fist, it's legal," and "Emotional abuse and neglect aren't crimes." Maybe what I'd been through didn't qualify as wrong?

It's not easy to admit to yourself—let alone others—that you've been abused. If you've grown up a certain way, or love your abuser as a spouse or family member, it's particularly hard to accept what's happened. Every time the abuser crosses a new line, we push our definition of abuse to something a little more extreme. We look at someone worse off and think, "I don't have it as bad as them, so I shouldn't complain."

But victimhood isn't a competition to see who has more suffering or deserves to express more trauma. The complexities of human emotion and spirituality defy summation in a whole library of books. One person may experience severe violence yet feel whole. Another may suffer years of hurtful words and feel like they're endlessly sweeping bits of their shattered heart off the floor of their soul.

Adding to the complexity, it can be difficult to differentiate an abuser from someone who struggles with sin but is genuinely sorry. I've found it deeply painful to come to terms with the fact that someone I love loves their sin more than they love me. It's agonizing to acknowledge that someone you admired is a narcissist, or a sociopath, or stubbornly and willfully dysfunctional. Confronting them with their sin, or cutting them out of our lives, feels like cutting off your right arm. It's heartbreaking and terrifying, and all your instincts scream against it.

I think that's largely why battered women sometimes stay with violent men. They love their husband, dad, boyfriend, or brother. It's easy to think, "What if he can change? Maybe he won't do it again? He seems sorry. Surely he'll get better if I stand by him and I'm good to him."

Sadly, by the time we realize he doesn't want to be good and isn't willing to change, we may be too afraid of him to leave. Making matters worse, the admission that our relationship was all a lie is humiliating, disturbing, and overwhelming. It feels unnatural to get help or leave. It's easier to pretend things aren't that bad. We make molehills out of mountains.

Abusers are often skilled at shifting blame, especially onto their victims. They're masters at making excuses. They trick people into feeling sorry for them. They may complain about their own traumatic childhood, or pass the buck, saying, "That wasn't me. The alcohol, the demons, the stress at work, or the utility bills made me do it." They may even deny events ever occurred.

I remember my dad apologizing to me once during my childhood, and that was because my mom threatened to tell our pastor after he'd left handprint-shaped bruises all over my 11-year-old body. During my early marriage, he apologized for many past traumas, but afterward, he'd pretend he didn't remember them happening and didn't remember apologizing either. The mind game was so glaring, and so distressing to me, that Jason told my dad to never communicate with me again.

Violence isn't the only kind of abuse. There are abusers who won't physically harm you, yet can make your life a living hell. Emotional abusers play convoluted mind games, manipulating and gaslighting until you don't know your own thoughts from their lies. Verbal abusers systematically insult and degrade, until all hope of joy is lost.

Narcissists gossip and spread lies, broadcasting your most personal secrets and making false accusations out of spite. They humiliate, seeking to damage your relationships with your spouse, friends, church, or employer—because once their victim is isolated and insecure, it's easier to manipulate and control them.

Like all people, abusers are far more complex than any doctor's diagnosis or psychiatric keyword. My dad's primary emotions were anger and depression. To him, love was sex and sex was hate. He fed his hatred with sadistic pornography, child abuse, mind games, and violent fits of rage. But he had good qualities too. On his best days he loved animals, he had a PhD in biology, and he taught at a university. He comprehended more academic theology than many pastors I've known, yet couldn't wrap his heart around a simple concept like compassion.

I've met a narcissist who, after being abused all her life, wore her damage proudly like a feather in her cap. She turned every situation into a convoluted plot to persecute her, leveraging the suffering of her own children to get attention and play martyr. She was an abuser, and also a victim.

I've met people who would give generous gifts, but then turn around and steal petty items, or intentionally break things and pretend it was an accident. Still others will flatter you to your face, only to insult and gossip about you later. Sometimes kindness is a camouflage, goodness a façade, and these superficial virtues enable abusers to infiltrate families, churches, and the hearts of the innocent.

IT'S COMPLICATED

Survivors are complicated too. None of us are perfect. Our lives are pockmarked with sins and mistakes. My own life has left little room for naivety. Riddled by pain and damaged by dark experiences, we may seem to act recklessly or illogically, yet do so out of hurt or fear as opposed to malice and ego. What appears nonsensical may make sense once the pain is traced to its source.

I've known a man who struggled to communicate his feelings because he assumed responsibility for the depression of his younger sister. He would rather believe he was a childhood bully than admit his mother had damaged her. In a needless effort to avoid hurting anyone else, he closed himself off emotionally.

I've spoken to men and women who, after being raped or sexually abused, went on reckless sprees picking up strangers at bars and attending wild parties. Some turned to alcohol, cocaine, or marijuana to numb their acute emotional agony. They'd wake up the next afternoon not knowing who they'd slept with or what they'd done.

I've known men who were mistaken by others as being misogynistic or sexist, but in reality had such poor self-esteem that they valued themselves based solely on their paycheck, sexuality, or outward appearance. They lashed out at women, presupposing judgment and rejection, but once you worked past their defenses, they were compassionate and grateful.

Despite their suffering, all these people came to regret their sin. They mourned their brokenness and fought to overcome. It may have taken years or even decades, but slowly and steadily they grew to understand their trauma, acknowledge their faults, and change.

Yet despite our good intentions, sometimes a fellow victim isn't healthy for us to be around. Sometimes we're not good for them either. We may bounce off each other's pain and trigger each other's trauma. Just because someone is a survivor doesn't mean you should allow yourself to be torn apart by their problems. Sometimes, the most loving thing we can do is entrust them to God, acknowledging them to be someone else's mission field. You cannot save a drowning person by letting them pull you underwater too.

The Bible is clear that all humans are capable of great good, and great evil. As the prophet Isaiah poetically put it, "We all, like sheep, have gone astray, each of us has turned to our own way" (Isaiah 53 v 6).

God plays no mind games and wastes no time sugar-coating facts. He confronts us with our natural propensity towards transgression. And while that's not a pleasant concept, deep down I think we all know it's true. We know we lose our tempers. We know we behave rashly. We know we say and do incredibly stupid things. We lie to ourselves, and we lie to others. We don't keep our own standards, let alone God's.

Everyone is a sinner. Not everyone is an abuser. Sorting all this out is complicated, because we are complicated. Sinful patterns and addictions may add layers of complexity to the already convoluted challenge of recovery.

Eventually, I had to ask myself: How can I discern who is trustworthy? How do I know I won't become an abuser? Is it safe for me to have kids? What if my dad was telling the truth: that his sin was my fault or I imagined it all? What if my dad passed on to me the propensity to abuse, like some hereditary spiritual disease?

GRACERS AND ABUSERS

I find it helpful to make a distinction between an abuser and what I call a "gracer." Here's the difference: abusers feed their sin, while gracers fight against it. A gracer may mess up, even horrendously—but they'll admit it, seek forgiveness, and actively change their thoughts, words, and deeds as a result. (Just to be clear, I'm not saying a "gracer" is necessarily a Christian—God gives what is often called "common grace," which restrains people from wrong choices, and influences them towards good ones, even if they don't recognize him or his activity. All of us, for instance, have a God-given conscience—Romans 2 v 14-16.)

A gracer will, upon reflection, admit their faults and authentically repent—turning their attitude and actions around. An abuser is often too proud and deceitful to genuinely apologize. If an abuser does apologize, it will be because they got caught, or to buy themselves undeserved trust, or to mess with your head.

A gracer will humbly work to improve. An abuser won't. They may appear to change or get better for a time, but eventually they'll return to their abusive ways. They're like the person Jesus describes in Luke 11 v 24-26, who, after being freed from an evil spirit, tidies up their soul with their own merit and pride, but is later repossessed to an even worse extent than before. So also, an abuser may clean up their act for a while, only to relapse back into worse sin than before. The book of Proverbs warns that "As a dog returns to its vomit, so fools repeat their folly" (Proverbs 26 v 11)— and this type of repeated folly has catastrophic effects.

By contrast, a gracer won't insist on cleaning up their act by themselves. They'll sacrifice their pride and accept help in order to mend a relationship. Abusers are rarely humble enough to seek counseling, because that would mean admitting weakness or fault. They insist they don't have a problem, or claim they'll fix themselves.

The difference between a gracer and an abuser is not always as clear-cut as hero versus villain, light versus dark, or Jedi versus Sith. You may find a tatted-up gracer in a bar at 2a.m., and an abuser sitting in a pew on Sunday morning.

So, how do we start to make the distinction between the two? Galatians 5 describes "the fruit of the Spirit," which is the collection of attributes that God grows in his people. But to help us in this context, it is also instructive in discerning generally between people who trend toward chronic sin and those who trend toward graciousness.

> *The fruit of the Spirit is love, joy, peace, patience, kindness, goodness, faithfulness, gentleness, self-control; against such things there is no law.*
> *(Galatians 5 v 22-23, NASB)*

Fascinatingly, abusers often exhibit the exact opposite behaviors to these.

Love vs. Apathy and Hate

An abuser doesn't love in the biblical, self-sacrificing sense. While they may claim to love, their style of relationship entails toxic levels of things like manipulation, control, obsession, addiction, deceit, guilt-tripping, narcissism, pride, and self-centeredness. They may not incorporate all those negatives, but they'll pick a few vices and hone them into an art form.

A gracer will love others more than their sin and pride. They'll be willing to make sacrifices for others instead of constantly demanding others make sacrifices for them. They'll actively try to maintain positive relationships and avoid hurting others' feelings. They won't dictate the aspirations and goals of others, but encourage their God-given talents and healthy desires, influencing them in positive directions.

Joy and Peace vs. Malcontentment

An abuser will have difficulty taking joy in things that don't feed their needs. They'll be insatiable, discontent, and endlessly longing for unattainable things. The more you try to please them, the higher they'll raise the bar. Your love will never be enough: not due to any fault of your own, but because they're an emotional black hole, always sucking but never filled.

A gracer will take joy in your accomplishments and talents. Your happiness will influence their happiness. They'll make you a priority and set aside time to be with you. Maintaining and building your relationship will bring them joy and contentment.

Patience vs. Impatience and Intolerance

Abusers often have little to no patience or empathy. Doing something outside their interests for the benefit of others is not their forte. They may be extremely patient when it comes to their own hobbies, but ask them to sit down and plod through something they don't enjoy, and you'll likely meet resistance. Many abusers are also bigots. They have a special place in their heart for tearing people down based on gender, religion, race, income level, or whatever. They are bitter, unsympathetic, impatient, and intolerant.

By contrast, a gracer may find your hobby boring, but they'll try it if only to spend time with you. They may even have some bigotry, but they'll come to recognize their bias as wrong and work against it. They'll forgive you for making mistakes and apologize for their own. They'll discipline their children out of love and not anger, help their spouse with projects and chores, and be capable of self-control.

Kindness vs. Selfishness

Selfishness could be said to be the hallmark of an abuser. They befriend people they think they can use. They puff themselves up at the expense of others. I've seen abusers seek out teaching positions in churches and schools, not because they love teaching, but because they enjoy having authority and undeserved trust. I've seen abusers live parasitically, frittering away their partner's paychecks while refusing to help around the house, parent the kids, get a job, or contribute anything positive to the relationship.

An abuser will leverage people who love them as a means to an end: to boost their ego, feed their deviant lifestyle, pad their wallet, or satiate sexual desires. An abusive parent may drown their child in responsibilities to make them feel inadequate, or neglect to teach them any responsibility to make them feel inept. When they seem like they're being kind, an ulterior motive is almost always at play.

A gracer, by contrast, is willing to serve. They enjoy caring for others, and desire to take their marriage to a deeper level. They consult with their spouse on big decisions, making them feel considered and respected. They won't withhold sex from their spouse in order to shame or manipulate, but they also won't insist on intimacy that their partner isn't comfortable with. They desire their marriage to be mutually fulfilling, not emotionally lopsided.

Goodness vs. Sin & Corruption

While a gracer will be ashamed of their vices, an abuser will willfully pickle their hearts in sin. They may superficially improve after counseling or correction, but only for a time, or only to continue in secret.

Abusers harbor and nurture their sin. In fact, their sin may grow so powerful that it becomes part of their identity. There's a catchy phrase, "Love the sinner, hate the sin," but the concept doesn't work when someone is so enamored with their dysfunction that it's become who they are. You cannot help a person who doesn't want to be helped. You cannot have a healthy relationship with someone who loves their sin more than they love you.

Faithfulness vs. Betrayal

Many abusers thrive on tricking people. They enjoy conning others into thinking they're kind, righteous, or trustworthy. They enjoy influencing and controlling, and what better way to control than to dupe someone into believing them?

Sexual sins are a common vice, so it's not surprising that abusers commonly make sexual deviance into a hobby. They may sexually abuse their partner, molest their own children, or betray someone's trust to sate their own desires.

A gracer may harbor a porn addiction or even cheat on their spouse. The difference is they'll regret their actions and feel shame. Most importantly, they'll repent and accept help to change, mature, and restore the relationship if possible. They won't expect or demand trust from people who they've hurt. They take loyalty and responsibility seriously, and thus take their sins and failures seriously too.

Gentleness vs. Violence and Harsh Words
Whether it's pummeling you with fists or bludgeoning you with insults, abuse beats you down. My dad's episodes of violence were often punctuated by months of depressive calm and ominous neglect. When he finally exploded, he'd throw things, smash glass, kick pets, and slam people into walls.

Once, when I was a teenager, my dad said I could go on a date. About twenty minutes before my boyfriend arrived, my dad changed his mind. He claimed he'd never given permission. He demanded I stay home. When I dared to argue, he picked me up—one hand gripping my arm and another my thigh—and he threw me half-way up the stairs.

I'd never felt so helpless. My head and shoulder hit the wall or the floor—I'm not sure which, maybe both—and I scraped my back on the handrail. He rushed up the steps, looming over me like an angry bear. I tried to slow my breathing so my panic wouldn't annoy him. I resisted the urge to cry because I knew tears would enrage him. I was quiet. I cowered. Eventually he walked away.

That's abuse. And yet, looking back, even worse than his violence were his hurtful words and sexual "compliments." I came to learn that bruises heal quickly, but a crushed spirit does not.

A gracer may also lose their temper. The difference lies in their reaction to their action. They feel ashamed by what they've done and avoid repeating it. They apologize, make amends, and desire to improve. They never retaliate against you for contacting a pastor, counselor, or the police. They take responsibility for their sin.

Self-Control vs. Recklessness and Greed

An abuser loves indulging their impulses. They resist moderating their behavior, except for the purpose of deceiving others or maintaining a public facade. They may only sin in secret, but the insatiable lust and reckless selfishness are there.

I can still see my dad, trembling with rage, bouncing on the balls of his feet, eyes wild and twitching because I left a book on the coffee table. He threw that book at my head. He also had no self-control when it came to his hobbies. During seasons of unemployment when my mom couldn't afford groceries, he'd buy pricey name-brand sports attire and ride his expensive new bike in style. He prioritized his wants over the needs of his family. He let his children go without while indulging himself.

By contrast, when I was about fifteen, I met a twenty-something man who seemed lonely and depressed. He had a dark background, I think. His hands tremored, and he bounced his knees compulsively. I met him at a coffeehouse where I played piano and sang. I developed something of a crush on him, and I guess he picked up on it.

One night, fixing his eyes on his beer bottle, he said, "We can never go out. I'm not good for you. Don't worry though. You'll find someone else."

In that moment he showed grace. He had a conscience and self-restraint. He saw a lonely, impressionable girl and didn't take advantage. Some might call it luck on my part, but I credit God and that young man with protecting me.

A PRESCRIPTION FOR TRUTH

An abuser probably won't exhibit all the vices in this chapter. They may act out periodically or abuse almost constantly. Just so, a survivor may have one traumatic watershed moment or have lived with abuse every day of their lives. While it's tempting for me to excuse my abuser, blame myself for his sin, or pretend my victimization wasn't that big of a deal, going back to this abuser/gracer dichotomy clears my mind of uncertainty.

Was I abused? Yes. Was my dad abusive? Yes. At one point I googled the legal term for one of his actions—one that I haven't described in this book. The title of the offense was so shocking to me that it was like a bucket of ice-water on my mind. It's painful to have your fears confirmed, but it's also relieving to know the truth.

You can't treat a wound until you realize you are injured. You can't see the light until you recognize the darkness. You won't recover from evil if you can't admit what evil is. God is a Savior who seeks out lost sheep, adopts orphans, and binds up the wounds of the crushed in spirit. There is no need to be afraid of the truth any longer. We can speak the truth, diagnose our pain, and accept a prognosis of hope. For when we call evil what it is, not only do we embark upon the process of recovery, but we deny our abuser power over our minds.

> *Abide with me; fast falls the eventide;*
> *The darkness deepens; Lord, with me abide;*
> *When other helpers fail and comforts flee,*
> *Help of the helpless, oh, abide with me.*
> *(Henry Francis Lyte)*

3. JESUS WEPT

He was despised and rejected by mankind,
a man of suffering, and familiar with pain.
(Isaiah 53 v 3a)

One of the most profound things God ever did was become man. Jesus suffered as man suffers, wept as man weeps, and died as man dies.

Why did he do this?

Primarily, to accomplish salvation for those who love him. Jesus lived a perfect life so he could credit his goodness to those who trust in him. He died an agonizing death so he could pay for our sins, in our place. He rose from the dead and ascended into heaven, so that his people could enjoy new life with him in heaven.

That's why God became man. But there was a secondary reason as well. God became man to assure us of his empathy and compassion. We know he understands our acutest pain, because he has felt it too.

JESUS WAS ABANDONED

The greatest king of Israel, David, wrote in Psalm 22:

My God, my God, why have you forsaken me?
Why are you so far from saving me,
so far from my cries of anguish?

My God, I cry out by day, but you do not answer,
by night, but I find no rest. (v 1-2)

About one thousand years after David penned his lament, Jesus quoted him from the apex of a blood-soaked cross. He groaned out the first four Aramaic words of the ancient poem: "My God, my God, why have you forsaken me?" (Mark 15 v 34). (And when you read Psalm 22 in its entirety, you will marvel at how poignantly it foretells his experience).

Now, the Son of God was not suggesting that his Father is an abusive father, nor a neglectful father. Jesus knew he was going to die before Adam and Eve bit into the forbidden fruit in the Garden of Eden at the beginning of human history (Genesis 3 v 6). Jesus is God. The Father is God. Jesus' life, death, and resurrection weren't just the Father's plan, but Jesus' plan too.

Christ humbly and willingly went to the cross because of his mercy, self-sacrifice, and dedication to his beloved people. Nevertheless, in that instant, as Jesus gasped his final agonizing breaths, torn by nails and scourged by barbed whips, he knew what it felt like to feel forsaken by a parent. He knew what it felt like to be abandoned, alone. Having always been unfathomably and gloriously one with God the Father and God the Spirit, he went to a place where they could not follow. He went to his death.

We can take comfort in knowing that God comprehends the indescribably bitter ache of being devastatingly separated from someone loved and needed. We can take comfort in knowing that God understands heartbreak and loneliness. As he hung bleeding and dying, surrounded by war-hardened Roman soldiers, a sadistic, mocking crowd, and vindictive religious hypocrites, Jesus knew what it was to feel truly unloved, brutally abandoned, and surrounded by hate:

Dogs surround me,
  a pack of villains encircles me;
    they pierce my hands and my feet.
All my bones are on display;
  people stare and gloat over me.
They divide my clothes among them
  and cast lots for my garment. (Psalm 22 v 16-18)

JESUS WAS BETRAYED

On the night of the Passover, the last supper he would celebrate with his friends before he died...

Jesus was troubled in spirit and testified, "Very
truly I tell you, one of you is going to betray me."
His disciples stared at one another, at a loss to know
which of them he meant ... Jesus answered, "It is
the one to whom I will give this piece of bread when
I have dipped it in the dish." Then, dipping the
piece of bread, he gave it to Judas, the son of Simon
Iscariot. (John 13 v 21-22, 26)

Have you ever wondered why Jesus told Judas he knew he'd betray him? Perhaps he wanted to give Judas a chance to change his mind. Perhaps he wanted to warn Judas against the evil he was about to commit. Perhaps he simply wanted Judas to understand the depth of his pain. Whatever the case, Jesus knew what was in Judas' heart, and he made that fact very clear to Judas.

Judas was one of the twelve disciples who followed Jesus everywhere, ate dinner with him, learned from him. Jesus washed Judas' feet. Yet Judas allowed sin to fester in his heart, which turned him against the man he called, "Rabbi," or "teacher."

Some conjecture that Judas betrayed Jesus for the bounty offered by Jesus' enemies—but that doesn't really fit the profile of a man who had sacrificed his home, job, and belongings to hike through dusty ancient Israel preaching, learning, and eating fish. Others theorize that Judas was hoping to frighten Jesus: to place him in a situation where he was forced to use his divine power to stop the crucifixion, overthrow the Romans, and free Israel. Still others suggest Judas was jealous: he wasn't the favorite disciple, the miracle-worker, or the guy Jesus helped walk on water.

Perhaps Judas simply saw the inevitable. Maybe he knew the religious elites who hated Jesus would eventually find a way to frame him. Rather than risk dying alongside his teacher, Judas negotiated to save his own skin. Whatever the case, Judas used sinful means to accomplish a sinful end. But all his conniving, scheming, lying, and gambling didn't save Judas. Rather, it drove him to despair, and he destroyed himself.

But Judas wasn't the only friend who left Jesus. Peter, one of Jesus' best friends, swore, "Even if I have to die with you, I will never disown you" (Matthew 26 v 35). Nevertheless, Peter denied knowing Jesus three times as Christ was tried and tortured. Upon realizing what he'd done, Peter broke down and wept. And by then, the other disciples had fled too.

Jesus experienced betrayal at the hands of those who had pledged loyalty and declared love for him. He understands how that feels.

JESUS WAS SLANDERED

Imagine Jesus' fake trial with me for a moment. Jesus is at the center—jeered, mocked, and falsely accused by liars wearing priestly robes. In the Old Testament, priests were appointed by God to speak for him to the people and offer him sacrifices on behalf of the people. They wore beautiful garments designed by and for the ultimate priest, Jesus Christ (Exodus 28 v 31-35). Talk about wolves in sheep's clothing! Even as they tortured and murdered the promised Messiah, these men wore his priestly robes. They sacrificed lambs in God's temple, even as they plotted to slaughter the Lamb of God on a criminal's cross.

The people Jesus loved and who he came to save called him a blasphemer—a liar, false teacher, and slanderer of God. They called him crazy. They called him a drunkard. They called him everything except what he was—the loving, patient, promised Messiah.

I have not been unfairly accused and unjustly condemned in a courtroom by my own people—but I was beaten in the living room where my family read the Bible and prayed. I know what it's like to be called crazy and a liar and told I'm the one who caused my abuser's sin.

Jesus knows what that feels like—what it's like to be lied about, to be the victim of vicious untruths and rumors, to have your reputation destroyed by selfish and powerful people.

JESUS WAS NEGLECTED

It would be an interesting exercise to count how many times Jesus was misunderstood, misinterpreted, or ignored. It might be easier to count the times he was understood.

Many times and in various ways, Jesus said he was the Son of God. Several times, he predicted he'd die for our sins and rise from the dead. Rarely was he understood, and frequently he was thought crazy or demon-possessed.

Even in the Garden of Gethsemane, as Jesus wept and prayed, anticipating his torture and death, his disciples unconcernedly fell asleep. Jesus said, "My soul is overwhelmed with sorrow to the point of death. Stay here and keep watch with me" (Matthew 26 v 38).

Now, if my friend told me, "My soul is overwhelmed with sorrow to the point of death," I'd be concerned. I hope I'd drop everything to comfort them, weep and pray beside them, even if I didn't understand what was wrong.

Jesus' friends did not do that.

As a kid I sometimes tried to tell people about my home life. Every time, I was misunderstood. I suspect they thought I was referring to normal parental discipline or maybe a weird one-off incident. I told them I was being beaten and worse in my own home, but they didn't take the time to listen or understand. Just so, the disciples had a wholly inappropriate reaction to Jesus' suffering. Instead of praying with him, wiping the sweat off his brow, and crying over his distress, they lay down in the grass and fell asleep (v 40, 43-44). And this didn't just happen once. Three times Jesus tells that his disciples his heart is breaking, but instead of caring, they take a nap.

What complacency. What disregard! How could they be so blind and apathetic? Yet, as I recall the many people I tried to tell about my suffering, who I tried to alert to what my father was doing to me, the disciples' reaction is all too easy to believe. Perhaps we're wired to do what's easiest rather than what's best. Perhaps human instinct is to block out what's uncomfortable or inexplicable. Perhaps we all by nature prefer to neglect people if to deal with their pain would upset the way we've been seeing life or risk the relationships or reputations we enjoy.

It's hard for most people to imagine that stories of abuse, like those you'd see on the news, could really be happening next door or in their church. Maybe it's simply too horrible to think possible. Maybe they don't want to know because then they'd have to care. Maybe intervening would be too messy or inconvenient. Whether their disregard is committed through ignorance and naivety, or irresponsibility and denial, the effect on the victim is a sense of isolation, neglect, and abandonment.

Abuse victims have a deep fear that if we break our silence, our words will fall on deaf or disinterested ears. If, like Christ, we tell someone, "My soul is overwhelmed with sorrow to the point of death, and I want to tell you why," but we're met with complacent responses like, "You should pray about it," or "Are you certain that's what happened?" or "I'm sure she didn't mean it like that," or "What did you do to make him lust that way?" all our fears are confirmed. And it breaks our hearts.

Sometimes when Jesus was not understood, he intended it that way. He chose to speak in parable stories so his meaning would be veiled. But often, Jesus spoke plainly, but was met by self-absorption, complacency, or worse. Just so, we may feel we're speaking a different language than everyone around us, or that nobody cares enough to listen or help. The resultant feeling of isolation is one Jesus knows very well.

JESUS WAS HATED

When my dad got angry, there was a terrifying silence before the storm. His face contorted, his eyes took on a vacant glare, and his whole body tensed and trembled as he bounced on the balls of his feet. What happened next was anyone's guess. He might break things, kick the dog, or throw dishes, books, or an iron at me. If nothing inanimate was at hand to grab, he might shove me against a wall, shake me, or throw me. While an outside observer might think, "He's out of control," I don't think there was anything out of control about dad. I think he knew exactly what he was doing and was completely self-possessed throughout his tantrums. From my perspective, his outbursts were not akin to the mindless punches and blathering insults of an angry drunk, but an explosion of hate and destruction which he thoroughly enjoyed. He sometimes laughed euphorically as he rampaged.

Have you ever seen someone so angry that they spat and trembled as they screamed at you? It's terrifying. This is how I imagine the angry crowds surrounding Jesus as the Roman governor, Pontius Pilate, who had final say over the life and death of every Judean, addressed the crowd. As was tradition during the Jewish Feast of Passover, one criminal was to be spared from punishment. Pilate gave the mob a choice between Jesus and Barabbas (Matthew 27 v 15-17).

Barabbas was a political upstart, violent rioter, and murderer. Pilate gave the people a choice between this extraordinarily undesirable criminal and a harmless rabbi, hoping they'd pick Jesus and solve Pilate's moral conundrum. However, the religious leaders stirred up the crowd, fomenting hate against Jesus. When Pilate asked the people if he should free Christ, the mob chanted, "Crucify him!" (v 22-23).

So, you see, Jesus knows what it's like to be hated.

What's stunning is that some of the people who chanted, "Crucify him!" in Pilate's courtyard may well have been souls for whom Jesus would die to save. The fact that a holy God was willing to humble himself, become mortal, suffer, and die for such extraordinarily undesirable people is testament to the greatness of his love.

That day, Barabbas was freed from the penalty of Roman law, despite being justly convicted, and the innocent, all-powerful Jesus was willingly condemned in his place. Just so, we too can be freed from the penalty of divine law. Our just conviction for ignoring and breaking God's commandments can be expunged. We can be freed because Jesus died in our place. He endured the wrath and judgment of God and man because he loved those who by nature hated him.

The insanity of hate is a terrifying thing. It's a murderous thing. It's a frenzy silencing reason, justifying injustice, and dulling the conscience.

My dad carefully behaved himself in contexts where he'd face consequences. He never lost his temper in front of people outside our immediate family. As a child, I was taught to be wary of doctors and police officers because they might lie about us, report us to Child Protective Services, and put us in foster care—where, I was told, we would be abused even worse.

That my father had the self-control to only go ballistic in private, and took measures to ensure we distrusted authorities, is one reason why I feel he understood his actions.

Just so, Pilate and the raging mob were in control of their actions. The religious leaders connived, premeditated, and plotted to stir up strife. Pilate washed his hands of the incident but could have stopped the execution had he wanted to. The irate chanting people had heard Jesus preach. They knew him to be a righteous man, yet they fell easily into the alluring lust of rage.

There is no pain, whether physical or emotional, that our God has not experienced. As David foretold in that ancient Hebrew song:

All who see me mock me;
they hurl insults, shaking their heads …
Dogs surround me,
a pack of villains encircles me;
they pierce my hands and my feet.
All my bones are on display;
people stare and gloat over me.
(Psalm 22 v 7, 16-17)

JESUS UNDERSTANDS

In Matthew 11 v 28-30, Jesus invites us:

> *Come to me, all you who are weary and burdened,*
> *and I will give you rest. Take my yoke upon you and*
> *learn from me, for I am gentle and humble in heart,*
> *and you will find rest for your souls. For my yoke is*
> *easy and my burden is light.*

Jesus does not crush us under the weight of rules and guilt the way a Pharisee or an abuser would. His yoke is not the law but the uplifting wings of grace. He does not threaten suffering and death if we fail to lead a pristine life. He lived pristinely for us. He carried the cross of condemnation in our stead. The only burden he requires that we carry is a love for him and a longing to be more like him.

We don't have a Savior unable to empathize with vulnerability, pain, fear, and limitations. Rather, we have a God who became like us: gnawed at by temptation, mocked by oppressors, humiliated, sorrowful, broken, and abandoned.

> *For we do not have a high priest who is unable to*
> *empathize with our weaknesses, but we have one who*
> *has been tempted in every way, just as we are—yet*
> *he did not sin. Let us then approach God's throne of*
> *grace with confidence, so that we may receive mercy*
> *and find grace to help us in our time of need.*
> *(Hebrews 4 v 15-16)*

Jesus doesn't shrug chickenheartedly as children are abused and sin ensnares us. Jesus reaches into the quicksand of our hopelessness and plucks us out of its trenches.

Jesus understands.

In 1 Samuel 1 we read about Hannah, heartbroken over her infertility, prayerfully begging God to give her a baby. Eli, the priest, saw her weeping but couldn't relate. Mistaking her for a drunk, he chided her instead of weeping with her. We do not have a priest who mistakes depression for sin or heartbreak for foolishness. Our God doesn't lack empathy or fail to parent his children. Our Savior comprehends our deepest pain.

Jesus wept.

Jesus weeps still.

Survivor, take comfort in this. God is not far away, disassociated, neglectful, or unseeing. He weeps with you, walks through darkness alongside you, and will carry you when you can't go on any longer. Only the God of the Bible has scars. Let them be a sign to you that you're never alone.

PRAYER

Lord, empower me to see my life in light of yours. Make me feel understood by you. Bless me with certainty that you sympathize with my agony. Fill me with gratitude and empathy for your suffering too.

4. CONCUSSION OF THE HEART

I am like the deaf, who cannot hear,
like the mute, who cannot speak;
I have become like one who does not hear,
whose mouth can offer no reply ...
For I am about to fall,
and my pain is ever with me.
(Psalm 38 v 13-14, 17)

The prolonged ache that won't go away. The sense of confusion, or feeling as if you're in a fog. Some memories are as clear as day, while others slip away as soon as you try to recall them. Some emotions sting acutely, while others feel muffled, muted, or even missing. The emotional dizziness, loss of trust, and tightness in your chest as you search for words to describe what you're not sure you feel or even want to understand.

This is a concussion of the heart—a trauma of the soul.

A FEELING OF FEELINGLESSNESS

Sometimes we don't realize we're in pain. Maybe we've been in pain for so long we've become accustomed it. Perhaps we've never not been in pain, so we think pain is normal. Often, we push our pain deep down inside in a futile attempt to feel or appear happy and strong.

This numbing—this suppression of emotion—can be a vital coping mechanism when someone is being abused. It gives us a broken sense of control at a time when we are out of control. It gives us insulation from the cruelty of an abuser, safeguarding our sanity through an ordeal that would rattle the strongest soldier.

But a problem arises when this suppression of emotion becomes habit, or even an ingrained facet of our personality. We feel out of touch with our own feelings, unable to tap into them. We have difficulty expressing ourselves, and may fear something is so intrinsically broken within us that we've lost our capacity to feel at all.

Even the most emotionally healthy and strong person, upon suffering a trauma, will exhibit behavioral changes. We adapt. We evolve. We compensate. We do what we must in order to survive. Perhaps we are not weak, but merely tired of fighting. Perhaps we are not broken, but stuck in defense mode.

The truth is, emotional suppression is not a sign that we lack emotions, but rather, that we've hit the mute button on them.

A feeling of feelinglessness is particularly common when we've experienced prolonged abuse. It's easy to see how disappointment after disappointment, betrayal after betrayal, and broken relationship after broken relationship, leads us to expect suffering. Unfortunately, when our primary examples of relationships—our parents, our families, our past marriages—are dysfunctional, it's easy to be drawn to more dysfunctional relationships either mirroring or contrasting what we know. It's also common to revictimize ourselves by entering relationships where we're at high risk of getting hurt or taken advantage of.

When I was a child, I was often told, "It's all in your head." I could be running a fever—and my dad would accuse me of lying, demanding that I complete my chores or homework. Once, when I had chicken pox, he claimed I was being a hypochondriac, exaggerating my symptoms or lying. He refused to let my mom take me to the doctor, even when I started having difficulty breathing.

This psychological abuse is sometimes called gaslighting, and was a consistent theme throughout my childhood and teen years. If I was angry, I was called dramatic. If my feelings were hurt, I was accused of PMS-ing, whether I really was or not. I was taught to ignore my feelings and view myself as a hypersensitive female. My emotions were treated as irrelevant, stupid, and imaginary. To this day, if someone offends me, I often bury my upset deep inside and refuse to address it. I fear being thought foolish or thin-skinned if I speak up. I worry that if I express myself, I'll be ridiculed, laughed at, or ignored, and wind up feeling even worse than I already do. Better to stay silent, or not feel at all.

One of my friends was badly beaten as a boy by his mother. If he cried, she would say, "Shut up and take it." She would punch him in the face repeatedly, raging uncontrollably. All the while, he learned to "take it," not complain, and hope that if he suppressed his cries she wouldn't beat him as badly. He learned that if he hid quietly in his room, she'd sometimes pass out from painkillers and leave him alone.

As a teenager, when he tried to tell people that his mother was violent—that he'd been beaten up by a woman—he was disbelieved or even mocked.

"I didn't fight back because I didn't want to hurt her," he told me. "If you defend yourself against a woman, they call you abusive, and if you don't, they call you weak."

So, he learned to bury his pain, suppress his sorrow, and choke down his fear. Society taught him to "shut up and take it," just as his mother had. This suppression became habitual, and part of his behavioral blueprint. It wasn't until much later in life that he was able to acknowledge his suppression and grow past it.

Another friend of mine bounced around in foster care before being adopted by an emotionally detached couple. He had several fathers throughout the years, one of whom was extremely violent. After being raped and suffering through a string of broken relationships and one-night-stands, he came, completely understandably, to believe that being alone was easier than being with people who supposedly loved him.

Our natural instinct, whether conscious or subconscious, is to reach for what we're used to, what feels familiar. This means some abuse survivors may not know how to feel loved unless someone is beating or berating them. We may have a completely inside-out and upside-down understanding of what love is. We may confuse love with sex, attention with manipulation, or dedication with jealousy. We may think devotion is when someone wants to control us. It is hard to establish and maintain a healthy relationship when we have no idea what a healthy relationship looks or feels like.

This is why I was so bewildered when my newly-wed husband, Jason, helped with chores. I'd never seen a man wash dishes without breaking them. In my isolated, broken world, men had three basic emotions: rage, depression, and apathy. I thought if my husband was doing housework, I must have failed somehow in my wifely duties. His work felt like my shame. His smile was confusing. I didn't know what to make of him. And I was terrified that he was secretly unsatisfied with me as a wife, and would eventually divorce me.

In other words, I interpreted my husband through the lens of my dad's dysfunctionality. When we're accustomed to responding to others in a defensive way, or translating our abuser's bizarre antisocial ticks to decipher what they really want from us, it becomes easy to misinterpret people who genuinely love us and want to help.

LEARNING TO FEEL AGAIN

Think of your emotions as levers that you pull in your brain to respond to the world around you. We all have them. If you're accustomed to pulling the Anger Lever, Defensive Lever, or Fear Lever, those may become your defaults. Your Anxiety Lever might be readily accessible, well-greased, and move with a smooth and easy whir, while your Happiness Lever might be rusted stiff and take an exhausting amount of effort to budge.

It's possible to grow so used to feeling betrayed, lonely, or distrustful that negative feelings are the only feelings you intuitively tap into. Meanwhile, other attitudes and emotions such as trustfulness, joy, confidence, and self-respect may feel awkward or unattainable.

We must give ourselves permission to feel. A life of numbness is mentally, spiritually, and physically unsatisfying. It inhibits our relationships, communication, and socialization. Worse, if we neglect to mend the cracks in our hearts, we may gradually begin to break down, slipping into depression, alcoholism, or other self-destructive behaviors that compound our struggle. Sometimes, as victims, we become so practiced at placating an abuser's emotions, we forget to even notice our own. The abuser's feelings were considered all-important, while ours were shunted aside. Learning to read our abuser's emotions became a survival skill, a way to map out emotional landmines and avoid them if possible. When someone is hyper-focused on defusing and dodging their abuser's emotions, they don't have time or energy for their own. Like a soldier on the battlefield, we develop a "Fight now, cry later" mindset. If you notice you're good at focusing on the emotions of others, but not on your own, therein may lie your problem. You don't lack emotions. You've simply lost track of them.

Once I was in the habit of walking on eggshells, it was very hard to stop. I had turned down the volume on my heart to mute the anger, fear, and anguish. The trick was figuring out how to turn the volume back up. If I wanted to stay home rather than go out, I had to learn to say so. If I was interested in a topic, I had to learn to bring it up, even if no one else did. If my feelings were hurt, even unintentionally, I had to learn to talk to the person responsible and make sure they knew. No matter how mundane or unimportant a feeling seemed to me, I had to practice expressing it.

Many survivors feel great trepidation about confiding in other people. If that's you, I'd suggest confiding in God first. Whether you close your eyes and pray, or write him a letter, he's by far the best listener I've ever met. Tell him about the numbing weight suffocating your emotions. Ask him to tap into what you've buried: to help you sense and express your feelings.

A woman recently asked me, "How do I pray?" I said, "Simply say, 'God...' and then talk." I've prayed with folded hands and closed eyes. I've prayed silently at the gym or aloud while driving to work. I've written my prayers like diary entries. However you pray, he wants to hear you. He sees all things, even the unformed thoughts of your heart. You don't have to have all the words right for God to understand you.

When a child learns to read, they start with the ABCs—the basics. When an athlete wants to bulk up, they start with small weights and gradually build to larger ones. Just so, if we want to learn to feel again, we must start with basic and small emotions. Nurture them. Start with what feelings you do feel. Exercise your ability to communicate them a little at a time. Once you're used to expressing smaller emotions, the larger ones won't feel as daunting. Be patient with yourself. Think of this as a strength-building process that takes practice and routine. You are establishing new emotional habits and a lifestyle of communication.

Another thing to do is expectation-set in realistic ways. If you come from a broken home, your concept of "happiness" may well be derived from television, celebrities, or people you only see on their best behavior at church or work. You want to feel like them, and be like them, and so you set emotional standards that are unattainable. The upshot is, no matter how much you heal, or how great life is going, you never feel like you're measuring up in the feelings department. You undervalue the positive emotions you do feel, because they don't look like the warm, fuzzy love expressed by Tom Hanks and Meg Ryan at the end of a chick flick, or the over-the-top joy of Ebenezer Scrooge when he finally understands Christmas.

Don't overlook your happiness because you're yearning for a level of feeling that isn't real. Rather, meditate upon the happiness you do feel, and nurture it so it can grow.

PERMISSION TO GRIEVE

What complicates everything is that, whether we want to admit it or not, we may also be angry at ourselves for being traumatized. Obviously, that's not fair, but logic rarely dictates emotions. Make sure you're not suppressing your emotions as a self-imposed punishment. Don't say to yourself, "You deserve to be treated badly," and leave your Self-Esteem Lever to rust in place. Don't lie to yourself, "You're too broken to be happy," and shut yourself off from friendship or love. Don't think, "You don't deserve to feel," and not feel at all.

Also, don't avoid emotions just because they're unpleasant. Hard work is often unpleasant, but consider the rewards. Give yourself permission to grieve. Grief is not one emotion but a multitude of conflicting and fluctuating emotions which may rush at us in waves or flow steadily like a current.

Everyone experiences and expresses grief differently. As survivors, we may feel angry that we were "weak," adamant that we are strong, ashamed that we were deceived, guilty that we "let it happen," terrified that we are vulnerable, or bitter that, even after years have passed, we're still dealing with the aftershocks of trauma. Some of us explode in an overwhelming flood of emotions. Others grow stoic and quiet, isolating themselves from others. Some feel constantly depressed, while others engage in risky behavior ranging from addiction to sexual recklessness and various forms of crime.

Grief can be all-consuming.

Grief will either define you, or you will define your grief.

If, like many of us, you're prone to express grief in dangerous or self-destructive ways, you can protect yourself by taking precautions and establishing healthy outlets. Finding ways to think through and process memories and emotions effectively is paramount. I'm sure you'll be unsurprised to hear that I process mine through writing. You can write your most personal, embarrassing, and harrowing secrets on paper and burn them. Watching those bad memories blacken, crumple, and vanish into carbon can be a cathartic way to lay them to rest.

We've got to be proud of our accomplishments, regardless of how insignificant they may seem right now. We've got to take pride in our recovery, measuring how far we've already come rather than how far we still have to go. We must embrace our emotions, especially the positive ones which we were taught didn't deserve recognition. We must show ourselves the patience our abusers did not.

THE WISDOM OF PRIVACY

Samson had a secret. He was a strong, hulking man, the terror of Israel's enemies, but he could be subdued if his secret weakness got out. Ignoring God's law, he allowed himself to become infatuated with a manipulative woman who worshiped different gods. Twice she sought to abuse his trust and betray him into the hands of men who wanted him dead. Even then, Samson did not leave her.

> Then [Delilah] said to him, "How can you say, 'I love you,' when you won't confide in me? This is the third time you have made a fool of me and haven't told me the secret of your great strength." With such nagging she prodded him day after day until he was sick to death of it. (Judges 16 v 15-16)

We know people such as Delilah exist today, but most of them are far more covert. A common reason we keep our stories to ourselves is fear of betrayal and judgment. Gossips, emotional abusers, cynics, and snobs love to wheedle out information they can use against us.

I've always been a talkative person, so when I finally came to terms with the fact that I'd been abused, I couldn't shut up about it. I'd held my secrets in so long that my newfound freedom of expression was intoxicating. I told friends at church, who didn't know how to begin to handle the information. I told relatives I shouldn't have trusted. I told total strangers in elevators. It was really embarrassing, but I didn't know how to stop.

You know those nightmares where you're out in public, look down, and realize you're totally naked? It felt like that.

I'd pour out my soul only to feel freakish and vulnerable later. Like the emotional suppression we previously discussed, this polar-opposite reaction is very common. In fact, survivors may pivot between the two, or experience a confusing combination of both, making us feel conflicted or even crazy.

One of my friends is a rape survivor. She was a child the first time it happened. Her trauma manifested in low self-esteem, and she had a string of sexual relationships with men who didn't love her. She was desperate for male protection and acceptance, but mistook sex for love. When she got pregnant, these men would bully her into having abortions. They coldly disposed of the consequences of their counterfeit love. They refused to protect those most in need of their protection: their own children and the mother who was bearing them. They completed their betrayal with the ultimate betrayal.

By the time she reached her thirties, my friend could stand on stage and go into intimate detail about her rapes with no more inhibition than had she been reciting multiplication tables. She had no privacy, no dignity, and no filter. Those mental barriers—the discernment which allows us to distinguish the intimate from the socially appropriate—had been eroded by her abusers. She thought she was being authentic and defiant, but she wasn't. She was exhibiting her vulnerability for everyone—including potential predators—to see.

Sometimes we subconsciously, but very intentionally, re-experience our pain in a context where we're able to feel in control. We rehash our traumatic experience, desperate to make sense of it, in a quest for validation. During my early twenties, at the ground-zero phase of my recovery, I had a frantic yearning to feel sane and accepted. I felt gawkish and inferior. I had kept my dad's secrets for two decades, but suddenly it felt as if one more day would suffocate me. Every time I told someone about my abuse, I caught another gasp of emotional air, before being dragged underwater again.

THE CULTURE SHOCK OF LOVE

Growing up, I thought I had a standard Christian family: that all men were like my dad and all moms were like my mom. I thought neglect was how life worked. Psychological, physical, and sexual abuse were the lifestyle I was born into. Abuse was my home, and I knew nothing else. It was normal.

When I married Jason, my world flipped upside down. Suddenly there was this man in my life who was kind, loving, and interested in what I thought. He cared about my feelings and was sympathetic and gentle.

Love hit me like a brick wall, and it hurt. I was horror-struck to realize by contrast what my father had been.

I went through a period of shock. Having been diagnosed with PTSD, I got to do fun things like breathe into a paper bag when I hyperventilated in public. It was miserable.

I became obsessed with getting everything out: my experiences, sorrows, nightmares, and brokenness. It was a mental purge. I had a dangerous urge to emotionally strip, exposing everything I was in hopes someone would love me enough to fix me and make me feel whole again.

I tried to be wise about who I confided in, but being diagnosed with PTSD made me second-guess my instincts more than ever, and I trusted some people against my better judgement. I asked my pastor to recommend a friend I could talk to. He suggested a woman who was also an abuse survivor. Unfortunately, she assumed I had the same issues she'd had at my age. She wrote an email, misinterpreting my feelings and accusing me of being afraid of men. To my mortification, she copied that email to my friends. I was crushed.

JENNIFER MICHELLE GREENBERG

I confided a good deal to a lesbian friend too. She was also a survivor, though her suffering was far more profound than mine. Unfortunately, things became awkward when she implied that I could be lesbian too, even though I was happily married to Jason.

I spoke to pastors and leaders who seemed to think I was an attention-seeker. One thought I was lying. Another thought I was crazy. I've heard horror stories of abuse survivors being sprinkled with holy water to cast out demons or being pressured to take medications for disorders they don't have.

Thankfully, I was blessed with a level-headed husband who had no desire to shut me up or drug me up. On a side note, medication can and does help many survivors cope with tempestuous emotions, at least until they get to a point where they can manage on their own. However, for people who aren't sick but have had a lot of sick things happen to them, medication is a temporary bandage as opposed to a long-term solution. It helps us cope in the interim, but it doesn't cure, and it cannot empower us to forgive or find peace.

I longed to take anti-depressants during the ground-zero phase, but Jason realized I was only depressed because I'd had a depressing life. He was certain that I'd get through PTSD in time, and he dedicated himself to supporting me through my recovery. It took one entire torturous year, and a lot of patience and love from him. Looking back, I can see that choosing to medicate or not were both acceptable options—merely different approaches to the same end. I suspect medication could have eased my recovery but may have prolonged the process slightly. Of course, every survivor's situation will be different. Choosing a course that's right for you is a personal decision, not a moral one.

Figuring out how to manage my trauma was an arduous process. Through trial and error, I came to learn how to identify trustworthy people who could humbly help me tackle my pain. Unfortunately, many survivors don't have a support system in place or counselors they can readily turn to. Finding a good person to talk to may be hard. I will say that seeking a therapist, pastor, or counselor who is noted for experience with abuse is your safest bet. I will also say that if your counselor seems questionable or makes you uncomfortable, leave. You don't owe them a second chance.

You may want to move to a new church, or for that matter, a new town. Removing yourself from constant reminders, painful situations, and awkward relationships is a major first step toward recovery. It's like getting out of the car following an auto accident.

BUILDING THE HOUSE AGAIN

As with any massive task, learning to process all this is easier if you share the load with others. It's what the Bible calls burden-bearing (Galatians 6 v 2). There are certain things only you can truly carry—it was your life, and your pain and grief (v 5). Yet sometimes, even knowing that someone else knows lightens the load inexplicably.

Imagine building a house. It might take years for one person, but a team of professionals could build it in months. Think of your emotional and spiritual defenses then as a house surrounding your heart. In addition to building your new emotional house, you've got to tear down your old broken house. You've got to purge all that pain, peel away the bad memories, absolve yourself of shame, and replace the damage with peace and love.

On your own, the process can be isolating and all-consuming. With supportive friends and knowledgeable advisors, the pain can be mitigated and not quite as lonely. Remember, God works through means. Looking back, I can see how he worked through many people—my husband, my friends, my pastors, and even some less than helpful people—to rebuild me brick by brick.

So, aim to build yourself a network of spiritual advisors, therapists, advocates, and doctors. Compare their advice, discuss it among them, and benefit from the whole gamut of their spiritual, practical, and scientific wisdom. Select people you trust, and, whenever possible, seek to benefit from spiritual and specialized knowledge for a holistic, whole-person approach.

Every step in your journey—even the painful ones—is progress away from that metaphorical car crash of your past. You may find a pastor you trust, but who is in over his head. You may be given poor advice, or trust someone who proves untrustworthy. Do not view these bumps in the road as failures but as learning experiences. If life were analogous to a math test, we could say that God does not grade us based on how many problems we face, or even how many problems we get right, but on whether or not we rely on him for help and solutions. Sometimes God will make the answer to our problem clear. Other times, he lets us puzzle and even struggle. These spiritual growing pains are no indication that he isn't sovereign or good. Rather, they are a sign that he is working in us.

> *Fear not, for I am with you;*
> *do not be dismayed, for I am your God;*
> *I will strengthen you, I will help you;*
> *I will uphold you with my righteous right*
> *hand. (Isaiah 41 v 10, ESV)*

5. DECONSTRUCTING SELF-DESTRUCTION

God is in control, and God is perfect—so we can let go of control, and we don't have to be perfect.

As finite and sinful creatures created in the image of an all-powerful God, it feels natural for us to strive after control we cannot hold. We're instinctively drawn to take charge, own responsibilities that are not our own, and worry over things beyond our control. Wrapping our heads around the concept that God is good and sovereign is a bitter challenge when our lives feel broken and chaotic. Nevertheless, like antiseptic on a wound, the truth that stings ultimately brings relief.

DENTING THE PLASTER

I don't remember why, but my husband and I were having an all-out yelling match. The more we fought, the more panicked I became. All my fears—of him leaving me, the constant self-berating in my head, and my deep-down belief that I'd never be happy—seemed to be converging and becoming true. I felt my sanity unraveling, the stress ungluing my last nerve, and I did it.

I bashed my forehead so hard into the wall that I dented the plaster.

Jason was shocked. I watched his expression change from disbelief to anger to fear in seconds. A voice in my head hissed, "You're too crazy to be his wife." He grabbed me in a full-body hug and held me down so I couldn't hurt myself again.

Honestly, that wasn't the first time I'd intentionally injured myself. I'd just never done it in front of anyone who cared before. When I was a teenager and my dad yelled at me, I'd sometimes throw myself against walls, slap myself, or slam my head into things.

Why?

For one, I needed to vent emotions too powerful and big for words to explain. But most of all, I needed to feel in control.

During abuse you're robbed of control. No matter what you do or how you plead, they keep hurting, harassing, frightening, and humiliating you. Your personal boundaries are violated, your will is denied, and your value as an individual is disregarded. You're terrified, pained, unable to make it stop, wondering when they'll let you feel safe again. All that matters to them is their emotions and desires. All that matters to you is survival.

Subsequently, when I found myself in high-stress situations—particularly ones involving anger but no physical contact—I'd add the missing element. I brought the violence by inflicting it on myself. It wasn't that I enjoyed suffering or wanted to perpetuate abuse. Rather, pain became something I could finally control. I'd been deprived of control for so long that I had an instinctive urge to assert my will and not enough self-worth to make self-harm distasteful. Thus, I became my own victim. I was used to being hurt and degraded, so hurting and degrading myself didn't feel wrong. In fact, it felt like home.

THE BROKEN CALM OF SELF-HARM

She had cuts all down her arms. Horizontal lacerations not deep enough to kill but severe enough to leave hundreds of thin white lines—like railroad tracks of scars.

"Why did you cut yourself?" I asked one day.

"It made me feel calm," she said, tugging her sleeve back down.

As abuse victims, we had about as much say over our fate as a lost astronaut drifting in space. The darkness isolating us in the vastness of our fear was a carefully concocted blend of danger, depression, and vulnerability. We were subjected to the whims of an abuser's mood, and lived in constant terror of treading on their emotional landmines.

Inflicting our own pain—being the one to hold the blade, slam the head, punch the wall, purge the stomach—is a way we can tell ourselves, "I'm in control. I own my own body. My abuser can't hurt me any worse than I can hurt myself. I'm just as powerful as they are."

Grasping that power is temporarily fulfilling and falsely reassuring. The result is a mirage of calm and an illusion of relief. We've channeled our emotional pain into our physical pain. Our sadness is now measured by the length of a cut. Our mental chaos is defined within the limits of a self-inflicted injury. Our pain can be started and stopped at will.

No matter how chaotic the world gets, how cruel other people become, or how out of control we may be in reality, at least we control this one little spot on our body. This section of arm, this face-sized dent in the wall, this terrible hangover from drinking too much—this is where we finally, desperately, despondently carve out a little piece of power.

RELIVING TRAUMA

Looking back, I've noticed my self-harm often replicated my dad's abuse. He used to slam me against walls, so I slammed myself against walls. He broke my things, so I broke my things. He hit me, so I slapped myself across the face. He said terrible things, so I told myself terrible things.

To my horror, I realized I'd taken on the role of an abuser in my life, and I hated what I'd become. I began to regret marrying Jason, fearing I'd condemned him to a life with my pain. I feared having children and making commitments. "What if I'm a monster? What if it's genetic or contagious? What if I damage my loved ones?"

But I am not my abuser. I have a choice. I aspire to heal and grow by God's grace. What motivated my self-harm was not a lust for abuse but a desperation for control. My mind was frantically grappling to find sense in the nonsensical.

I've witnessed this pattern in the lives of many survivors. The child of an addict will sometimes relive childhood horrors by becoming an addict themselves. A rape victim may pick up strangers at bars, replicating high-risk sex devoid of love. A person abandoned or homeless as a teenager might repeat a pattern of abandonment in serial failed or sabotaged relationships. Some might assume we're so used to pain we don't know how to live without it. While this sounds plausible, I don't think it's always the case.

Rather, I think we yearn to make sense of our pain. We want to understand what our addicted parent was going through, so we subconsciously recreate what they did to their souls in our own. We unintentionally re-enact the situation in which we were hurt, in hopes that this time we'll find a way out. We feel a need to study, analyze, and understand our suffering. Our life becomes an unintentional series of doomed laboratory experiments in which we're the scientist and the rat. When our quest for answers involves a self-destructive research process—recreating and re-experiencing our pain or the sins of others—we get caught in a cycle of self-harm. We undertake exhaustive testing yet find no solutions.

Whenever I see self-destructive patterns in my life, I follow the river back to its source. I follow my pain back to the original trauma. I search for similarities in order to understand why I'm doing what I'm doing. While it may appear erratic, my behavior is rarely random. Our emotions follow patterns just like the blood vessels leading to our hearts, then back out to our fingers and toes. Just so, I can trace my pain back to its heart. Once I connect the dots, pain's power begins to fade.

SELF-NEGLECT

One of the toughest emotional challenges I've faced is my tendency toward self-neglect. Under the pretense of saving money or time, I'll neglect to eat, buy new clothes, cut my hair, or take care of myself. Sometimes it's intentional, but usually it's subconscious. This too is a kind of control, a self-inflicted brand of pain. I'm regulating my joy, micro-managing my self-worth, and depriving myself of necessities the way an anorexic deprives themselves of food. I must follow the river back to its source.

As the oldest of five siblings much younger than me, I felt very maternal and protective of them. I tolerated my dad's abuse, hoping he'd leave them alone. If there wasn't enough food, I'd go without so they could eat more. If I earned money babysitting, I often spent it on necessities or gifts for my sisters. I didn't want them to go without, so I went without instead, and that made me happy.

This behavior became so ingrained that even today I find doing nice things for myself to be stressful and depressing. I hate spending money on myself, partly because I'm used to being frugal.

My dad would sometimes be unemployed for nearly a year at a time. He was anti-social and intimidating. Once, he caused a ruckus because he didn't want a female manager.

Whenever an employer downsized, he was on the chop-list. But even when we did have money, it often wasn't spent practically. There were times when I was wearing pass-me-down mom-jeans, while dad spent thousands of dollars on a high-end bicycle, pricey clip shoes, and name-brand athletic apparel. I remember my mom coming home from the grocery store weeping because she couldn't afford milk. That afternoon I made $1 boxes of Kraft mac-n-cheese using water. But our fridge was always stocked with dad's beer.

This tendency to indulge himself while his family ate watery box dinners and wore decade-old clothing was, I think, part of my dad's psychological abuse of us. He was valuable. We were not. He was worth splurging on. We were what charity was invented for. He was entitled to have pricey hobbies and blow money while unemployed. We were to go without, stroke and compliment his shaved cyclist legs, and never ever complain. I drained that cup of lies to the dregs, and it shows whenever I neglect myself. "I'm not worth it," I think as I skip lunch. "I'm in control."

PEOPLE-PLEASING

As a child, one of my friends was forced to strip naked on the back porch every day after school. Upon opening the door, he and his brother would find a trail of newspaper protecting their mother's pristine flooring. They'd follow that trail to the bathroom, where they'd wash and decontaminate themselves.

His mother never physically harmed him, but psychologically she devastated him. He was taught that he was disgusting, that he could never be good enough, and that her pride as a housekeeper was more important than his feelings. His value as a person was defined by her opinion of his hygiene.

You might imagine that as an adult he would have become obsessively clean or germophobic. But he didn't.

Rather, he became a workaholic overachiever. Much later, he realized he was emotionally enslaved to the opinions of others.

This is called people-pleasing. There are religious mutations too, sometimes called works-religion or legalism. This slavery to the approval of others can resemble self-righteousness and pride, or even virtue and kindness, but never underestimate the self-loathing at its core. Our hearts become enslaved to the opinion of another. We must do, do, do to prove we're good, better, best—endlessly striving after an unachievable ideal.

Being an overachiever is often touted as a virtue, but when it springs from shame and emotional deprivation, it's damage. Like a penitent monk whipping his back raw, we beat ourselves up emotionally. We strive to be the best, to impress people who don't care, and we bend over backwards to go above and beyond. We may work excessive overtime, parent our kids to be prodigies, excessively regulate our diet, and so on.

Abusers teach us to fearfully obey. They demand we meet impossible standards. While their rules are often arbitrary, they give a false sense of structure and hope in an otherwise chaotic environment.

Paul taught, in Romans 6 v 16, "When you offer yourselves to someone as obedient slaves, you are slaves of the one you obey." John Calvin, the sixteenth-century Reformation pastor, concurred, noting how "the human heart is a factory of idols." We enslave ourselves to all kinds of things, from other people's opinions to projects at work to our own to-do lists. But there's only one Master, as Paul puts it, and if we're going to obsess over pleasing anyone—if we're going to be enslaved—it should be the Savior who loves us, and requires nothing but love in return.

Now that you have been set free from sin and have
become slaves of God, the benefit you reap leads to
holiness, and the result is eternal life. For the wages
of sin is death, but the gift of God is eternal life in
Christ Jesus our Lord. (Romans 6 v 22-23)

Claiming Jesus as our Lord and Savior means we're no longer enslaved by rules and shame, but we're now heirs of forgiveness, acceptance, and grace. We can stop being good so others will love us, and start being good because we love God.

In order to break the cycle of self-harm, self-neglect, or people-pleasing, we must first let go of what we never had: control. That means our abuser's control, our own control, and even our control over our abuser.

STEP ONE: REVOKE YOUR ABUSER'S CONTROL

For years I maintained a controlled, limited relationship with my abuser. I hoped to help him. I dreamed of a day when he could be a good dad and grandpa. However, after enduring a real-life soap-opera of painful betrayals and exhausting conflicts, I realized I couldn't fix him. He'd inch his way past boundaries I'd set, or simply invent new ways to manipulate or hurt me.

When we try to control our relationship with an abuser, we actually give them control over us. Everything we do starts revolving around controlling their control over us. If you had putrid trash in your kitchen, you wouldn't get rid of the smell by scooting it into another room. You'd take the trash to the curb, out of your home, and out of your life completely. Just so, if an abuser won't stop abusing, you are justified in removing them far from you.

If our self-harm is a broken attempt to control, then revoking our abuser's control is the first step toward overcoming. Denying them influence over our schedule, activities, lifestyle, relationships, opinions, and wellbeing removes them from the driver's seat of our hearts. It denies them power and consequently it empowers us. It lessens the risk of us harming ourselves, because it removes the motivation for our desperation.

STEP TWO: RELINQUISH YOUR CONTROL

There are some things we can control to a healthy degree. For example, I manage my anxiety by running. It's a simple thing I can take pride in and call my own accomplishment. I have friends who play guitar, lift weights, or do scrapbooks, all for the sake of carving out a little piece of peace. In the grand scheme of things, however, what we can control is a drop in the ocean.

You and I are finite and faulty. Some would have us believe that we control our destiny, but the truth is, none of us controls even one hair falling from our head, let alone the actions of others. Ultimately, you and I aren't in control, and that's a good thing. The wisest people know they aren't wise, and therefore aren't equipped to hold the reins in their lives. Someone like me, who's been known to literally bang her head against a wall, is not qualified to chart the course of her life. Sure, I can nudge it in positive directions; I can apply for that job, lead a healthy lifestyle, and be kind to others. But I don't know the day I will die. I am not in control, and the great news is, I don't need to be.

STEP THREE: ACKNOWLEDGE GOD'S CONTROL

When we make-believe we're in control, we crush ourselves under a too-heavy burden. Rather than struggling to fill a role I'm clearly ill-suited for, I've learned to rest in the knowledge that God is in control. He's not in control the way a tyrannical abuser is in control. He's sovereign in the way a loving parent wants to help and teach, a doctor loves to cure and heal, and a shepherd gently guides and protects. He is a sovereign Savior who toiled to rescue and redeem.

In Luke 12 v 6-7 Jesus says:

> *Are not five sparrows sold for two pennies? Yet not one of them is forgotten by God. Indeed, the very hairs of your head are all numbered. Don't be afraid; you are worth more than many sparrows.*

If God notices when a frail baby bird falls from her nest, he knows when you're weak or in need. The Lord who orchestrates planets and sets every star in orbit is powerful enough to heal your spirit. The Creator who strings together atoms and DNA does not consider your worries and struggles too small to care about.

Ultimately, control belongs to God. This is his world. He made us, and we are his. Thousands of years ago, when Job responded to his affliction by suggesting God was being unfair, God responded:

> *Where were you when I laid the earth's foundation?*
> *Tell me, if you understand.*
> *Who marked off its dimensions? Surely you know!*
> *Who stretched a measuring line across it?*
>
> *(Job 38 v 4-5)*

And Job responded:

> *I know that you can do all things;*
> *no purpose of yours can be thwarted.*
> *You asked, "Who is this that obscures my plans without knowledge?"*
> *Surely I spoke of things I did not understand, things too wonderful for me to know. (42 v 2-3)*

Job came to understand that not only is God in control, but that his control is "wonderful." As survivors, it can be terrifying to entrust our fate to another, even though, deep down, we know we don't control our fate anyway. So, here's our comfort: God uses his control, his power, for our good:

For God so loved the world that he gave his one and only Son, that whoever believes in him shall not perish but have eternal life. (John 3 v 16)

And when we find we don't know how to trust God, we can ask God to give us trust. He is sovereign over everything, even our hearts. Like the father of a boy suffering from an evil spirit in Mark 9, we cry out to Jesus, "I believe; help my unbelief!" (v 24, ESV).

A. Jesus Followed All the Rules

Jesus didn't die for us because we're wonderful and perfect. He was wonderful and perfect, and so he could die—and chose to die—for us. During the mid-1700s, Charles Wesley penned the hymn "And Can It Be?" Read these lyrics from the fifth verse, which I've adapted to modern English:

No condemnation now I dread.
Jesus and his righteousness is mine,
Alive in him, my Advocate,
I'm clothed in righteousness divine.
Bold I approach his eternal throne,
And claim my crown through Christ my own.
Amazing love! How can it be
That You, my God, would die for me?

If the perfect life of Christ is sufficient to satisfy a holy God, surely it's sufficient to satisfy us. Too often, we align our standards with those of our abuser rather than with God's. However, our abuser's standards were illogical and changeable, and based on their moods rather than morality or love.

Substitute God's grace for your abuser's expectations. God isn't going to scream at you for asking too many questions. He won't beat you up for loading the dishwasher wrong. Your faults and failures, real or imagined, great or small, are no match for his irresistible mercy. He lived a perfect life, so you need never feel like a disappointment again. Through faith, his perfection is credited to you, so you need never feel like you have to measure up; so you can let go of the weight of trying to earn his favor.

Accept Christ. Accept that right now Jesus, the Son of God, is praying for you. God desires your recovery. Your value as an individual has nothing to do with your abuser's opinion of you, or even your own opinion of you. It has everything to do with God's opinion of you, and he loves you more than any human being is ever capable of comprehending.

You don't need to crucify yourself to feel paid-up or at peace. Take yourself down off that cross. Remove the crown of shame from your head. It's not your job to pay for your sins if Jesus has paid for them for you. You don't need to be in control, because Jesus Christ is sovereign.

B. Jesus Is Sovereign

> But you, Sovereign LORD,
>   help me for your name's sake;
>   out of the goodness of your love, deliver me.
> For I am poor and needy,
>   and my heart is wounded within me …
> I am an object of scorn to my accusers;
>   when they see me, they shake their heads.

*Help me, L*ORD *my God;*
save me according to your unfailing love.
Let them know that it is your hand,
*that you, L*ORD*, have done it.*
(Psalm 109 v 21-22, 25-27)

In this poignant psalm, David acknowledges God's sovereignty. He admits he's helpless and wounded in heart. His accusers have spread lies about him. They shame, mock, and condemn him as worthless.

Yet David doesn't say, "But actually, I'm an awesome guy and everyone should admire me!" or "I'm a powerful king and will prove my worth." Rather, David resigns himself to his neediness and asks his sovereign Lord to validate him—not because of anything good David has done—but because God is unfailingly good, loving, and in control.

Survivor, you have nothing to prove. God doesn't value you because you are perfect. He values you because he is perfect. He doesn't "help those who help themselves." The Bible describes God as the Father of the fatherless and Helper of the helpless (Psalm 68 v 5). We can cast off our burdens of shame, self-harm, perfectionism, and people-pleasing. We can surrender our futile struggle for control, which is grasping after wind. We can rest knowing God is sovereign and God is good.

STEP FOUR: YOU ARE NOT YOUR PAIN

It's easy for us, as survivors, to wear our damage like a soldier's uniform. It's something to be defined by, gives us a sense of safety in numbers, and helps us fill a role we think is expected or deserved. Our damage becomes our identity, our sense of who we are—and so it remains our burden. This is why the Bible encourages us to put off our old ways and put on the ways of God, as if we're putting on fresh, clean clothes:

You were taught, with regard to your former way of
life, to put off your old self, which is being corrupted
by its deceitful desires; to be made new in the attitude
of your minds; and to put on the new self, created
to be like God in true righteousness and holiness.
(Ephesians 4 v 22-24)

Just so, we can put off this degrading and depressing way of life. It will take time, and it will be a process, but we can take off these old behavioral patterns, and put on new patterns which build us up and bring us joy. We can recognize our negative tendencies and emotional ruts. And as we consider how our behavior—whether self-destructive, legalistic, self-neglecting, or overachieving—might be an attempt to grasp control, we can rely on God to love us through it all. We can find the pattern and break the pattern. We can put on our new identity in Jesus Christ.

I know that my Redeemer lives;
What comfort this sweet sentence gives! ...
He lives to silence all my fears,
He lives to wipe away my tears,
He lives to calm my troubled heart,
He lives all blessings to impart. (Samuel Medley)

6. THE PROBLEM OF GUILT
(AND THE ANSWER TO IT)

*Even if I were innocent, my mouth would
condemn me;
if I were blameless, it would pronounce me
guilty. (Job 9 v 20)*

One of the most tragic after-effects of abuse is the survivor's profound guilt and frantic desperation to explain it. I think we all feel this guilt, this shame, to one degree or another. I've spoken with the neglected children of alcoholics, women who were raped as adults, men who were beaten senseless as children, and people who survived their teen years by running away. Regardless of the type or severity of abuse, we've all felt—and oftentimes still feel—that gnawing ache, that sickness in the pit of our stomach.

I've found it helpful to break things down into two types of guilt: Borrowed Guilt, which is when we feel responsible for things that aren't our fault, and Legitimate Guilt, when we really did say something hurtful or do something wrong. There is hope and healing for both.

A BURDEN WE SHOULD NOT CARRY
"Why didn't I do something?"
When I was a young teen, my friend Misty, a pastor's wife, used to take me to movies or lunch. I never told her about

my dad's anger or perversion. I loved our outings and wanted them to stay pure; free of drama and weirdness. I feared I wouldn't be believed, but most of all, I feared I would be believed. You see, if she believed me, she'd tell her husband, who would confront my dad, who would be furious. I feared they'd get the police involved, and if CPS took me away, my siblings would be separated, and I might not see Misty again. Plus, how do you tell someone that your dad is a monster who has them fooled? So I stayed quiet. This led to the gnawing questions of "Why didn't I do something? Had I spoken up, would things be different? Would we be happier?"

Often, we feel guilt over things we didn't do and couldn't prevent. On some level we may realize we shouldn't feel guilty, but that only increases our confusion. It makes us feel foolish, illogical, and weak. We begin to question our ability to reason, and we distrust our emotions. It's tempting to smother this Borrowed Guilt, because it feels illogical yet hurts so bad.

"Why did I cooperate?"
It's not unusual for children and teens to want their sexual abuser to find them attractive. Kids naturally want to impress. They strive to please. Think about all the times you worked diligently on a new refrigerator art piece, or history report, or practiced hard to get on that sports team.

That same instinct is at play here.

As a teenager, I desperately wanted my dad to think I was beautiful. A good dad will compliment his daughter and build her up. Girls need encouragement, and there's nothing wrong with desiring it. It wasn't my fault that my dad's concept of beauty for his own daughter was perverse and sexual. He set the bar. He defined the standard. Who was I, as an adolescent, to discern his priorities or compliments as warped? He was my dad and I loved him. I trusted him to want what was best for me. As a child, I asked myself, "Why do I feel flattered? What's wrong with me?" As an adult, I realize my dad took advantage of my innocence and natural desire to please him.

"What if I'd done something differently?"
I remember coming home from the mall and proudly showing my mom the new tankini dad had bought me. Instead of the smile I anticipated, her face went white.

"She's a young girl," she said to him. "I'm not ready for men to look at her like that."

"She's 15," he retorted. "It's no big deal."

Instantly I felt ashamed. "How could I be so foolish? I should have told dad this was a bad idea, but we were having fun. Now they're fighting, and it's my fault. My body causes sin. I'm disgusting."

If I could feel guilty over small things, I could shred my heart over larger things. I dearly wished I could turn back time and stop bad things from happening. I wanted to manage my abuser's emotions and heal his brokenness, but that was outside my control.

No matter how much we guilt-trip ourselves, it won't change the fact that we're not in control. We never were. It's tempting to imagine "What if?" but doing so only inflicts pain on our already pained soul. We cannot go back. Even if we could, our abusers would still be abusers.

THE GUILT-TRIP EFFECT
When I was about 12, my family lived on several unfenced acres in the country, surrounded by ranchland and miles of juniper trees. One summer, our dog went into heat, and a neighbor's male dog began trespassing into our yard. That evening, as I was setting the dinner table, my dad arrived home from work.

"That damned dog is in our yard again," he said. "Should I shoot it?"

I laughed incredulously.

"Sure dad," I joked. "Shoot the neighbor's dog. That's a great idea."

He got a weird glint in his eye and rushed to his bedroom. Suddenly it dawned on me he might not be joking. As I followed him into the bedroom, he pulled out his 3.57 magnum, and blew the dog's hind legs out from under it. The dog twisted in the air and bounced against the dirt before shrieking away on three legs. My little sisters, who were around six and eight, began to cry.

"Did you shoot that dog?" my mom screamed. Dad put away his gun, retrieved an edition of Berkhof's *Systematic Theology*, and walked silently into the living room.

I hovered about for a few minutes, trying to gauge his mood. Once he looked safe, I asked, "Daddy, why did you do that?"

He let his book drop, feigning confusion.

"You told me to," he said, and then went on reading.

You told me to. You made me do this. It's your fault.

My dad was blame-shifting. In this instance, it was so obvious that even my 12-year-old self was taken aback. Most guilt-tripping is more cloak-and-dagger. Children have a natural inclination to trust adults, especially their parents. And we all—adults and children—have a deep desire to believe the best of those we love. Abusers often take advantage of this.

They blame their victim for their rage and cruel words. They say we should have done better cleaning the house, performing in the bedroom, or earning a bigger paycheck. They may blame you when your dog dies, suggesting you could have taken better care of it; or when the car needs repairs, because if you'd maintained it differently, clearly it would last forever. They may blame you when dinner burns, measuring your value as a human being by the tenderness of a chuck roast. They may blame you for not having any friends, while simultaneously demanding all your attention. There are a million petty, intimate, and malicious ways abusers use to make their victim feel ashamed. The more ashamed we feel, the less likely we are to report. The longer we wait to report, the more foolish we feel doing so.

Being blamed on a recurring basis has a wearing effect. Like an ocean beating against a shore, an abuser's insults and accusations gradually erode our sense of self-confidence, dignity, and independence. What we initially chalked up to "lack of sympathy" or a "temper" evolves into full-blown abuse. We're constantly bracing ourselves for the next attack. It's exhausting. And the more exhausted we become, the more vulnerable we are to manipulation.

As their lies get bigger and more ridiculous, the smaller lies start feeling believable by comparison. We grow accustomed to being blamed and second-guess our own judgement. Our abuser's accusations begin to auto-populate in our heads. Once we distrust our own reason and emotions, we're far less likely to act upon our distrust of our abuser. If we can't depend upon ourselves, they gamble we'll depend on them.

BORROWED GUILT

We are born into a state of naive trust. As children, when we're corrected, our natural instincts tell us, "I'm young. I don't understand everything. I must have done something wrong, and I shouldn't do it again." This is the natural thought process of small children. We genuinely don't know. We desire to please our parents. So, when grown-ups give confusing, warped directions, wires get crossed and emotions get twisted in knots.

As the mother of three young children, I must explain that scissors are sharp, climbing shelves is dangerous, and the stove is hot. Imagine that power in the hands of an abuser. They can easily teach us that being beautiful is shameful, that their anger is the direct result of how obnoxious we are, and that our laughter is a beat-worthy offense. Parents hold immense power over the psychological development of their kids. They can fill their minds with empowering love or corrosive pain; feed them divine truths or toxic lies. They can build them up virtue by virtue, or chip away at their souls until there's no hope left inside.

Kids believe what they are told. If kids can believe in Santa Claus, they can believe in their own worthlessness. It's not that they're stupid, but they're innocent. Shame is a far easier sell than flying reindeer, and abusive parents are skilled at spinning lies.

If you're a child-abuse survivor, your abuser took advantage of your trusting child-mind, betraying you on an intrinsic level that defies understanding. Looking back with your adult-mind, you may start to view circumstances, words, and actions from a mature perspective. You may wonder, "Why didn't I tell someone? Why didn't I ask them to stop? Why didn't I run away? Why did I enjoy that kind of attention? It's my fault."

But the fault is theirs, and theirs alone.

Don't disregard your child-mind. Don't project your adult reasoning onto the heart of your youth. Remember the trustfulness and naivety you had. As adults, we tend to lose sight of that beautiful, pure, child-like heart, hungry for love. We were trusting, unsuspecting, and striving to please. There was a time when the worst monsters we could imagine hid under our beds or skulked in dark closets. There was a time when our daddies were superheroes and our moms were the kindest, prettiest ladies in the world. There was a time when we wanted to be astronauts, cowboys, veterinarians, and princesses. Imagination and hope ruled because practicality hadn't settled in yet. We tend to place our adult-self into the shoes of our child-self and wonder why we reacted the way we did. It's a dangerous mistake, and likely where much of our borrowed guilt is rooted.

As adults, we don't let our parents take our clothes off. As young children, it was normal. We couldn't tie our shoes, button our shirts, or put our pants on without falling over. Children trust their parents implicitly. There's no understanding of sexuality, let alone perversion. Because of this naivety, when something sexual does happen, a child may not realize anything is wrong.

When I look back to one particular event when I was very young, I remember my dad's eyes. My child's mind thought he looked worried or sad. I feared I'd done something bad, or he'd seen something wrong with me. I didn't understand. With my adult mind, I perceive what he did as shocking, humiliating, and wrong. How did I not understand when I was a kid? It's because *I was a kid*. He was my daddy. I was his baby girl. Don't blame yourself for thinking like a child when you were a child.

Often, when we recall our darkest memories, we also recall our feelings. There may have been awkwardness, fear, or a longing for admiration. There may have been a sensation we later came to understand as arousal or even orgasm. While our bodies may have been capable of stimulation, our minds revolted against it, and our souls were thrown into a state of profound confusion.

Desperately, we grasp at straws trying to explain why we weren't loved, why we didn't understand, and why we reacted the way we did. But no matter how naively we behaved, or what we were manipulated into doing, the guilt is not ours. It's theirs.

LEGITIMATE GUILT

As imperfect people, we sin. When our sin coincides with our victimization, it leads to much confusion. We may have ulterior motives, feel vindictive, or wish harm upon those who harm us. When our abuser accuses us of sins we can imagine committing, or have committed before, we do a double-take, questioning our hearts.

Maybe we really were trying to irritate them. Maybe we lied to avoid some undesirable task. Maybe we've cheated on our violent spouse or found solace in a bottle rather than God. We're human. We're sinners. We make poor choices and do bad things. This is legitimate guilt—things that really are our fault. This guilt is the healthy response that conscientious people have when we know we've done something wrong. However, our sins and failings in no way excuse our abuser's sins and failings. Our guilt isn't a get-out-of-jail-free card for them to whip out, eliciting our silence. We are not responsible for their choices and behavior.

This is a tricky balance as a survivor. However, for the sake of breaking free of guilt and recovering, it's a balance worth striving for. We must reject Borrowed Guilt and hold abusers accountable, while simultaneously being honest with ourselves about our own sin and Legitimate Guilt. The Bible is clear:

> *There is no one righteous, not even one … all have sinned and fall short of the glory of God.*
> *(Romans 3 v 10, 23)*

But while we're all sinners, some are worse than others, and the evil of abuse falls squarely on our abuser's heads. No matter what we have done—or not done—nobody deserves to be abused. The Old Testament prophet Ezekiel said:

The child will not share the guilt of the parent,
nor will the parent share the guilt of the child.
The righteousness of the righteous will be credited
to them, and the wickedness of the wicked will be
charged against them. (18 v 20)

I remember in my teens watching the news with my dad. A female commentator observed forcefully, "I don't care if a woman cartwheels through Central Park naked at two in the morning; she doesn't deserve to get raped." Her remark made a huge impression on me. She'd unwittingly helped a teenage victim understand that her abuser's sin wasn't her responsibility.

Eventually, I told God everything I felt guilty over. Embarrassing things. Humiliating things. Evil things that weren't my fault. I confided in God and begged him to ease my conscience: not because I was necessarily guilty, but because I was too riddled with shame and confusion to sort my Borrowed Guilt from my Legitimate Guilt.

At a time when my dad should have been teaching me how to cut out paper dolls, he was teaching me how to cut my wrists. It was knowledge I should not have had from a source I should never have received it from. I thought I must be defective for my own dad to feel the need to educate me thus. I think I was experiencing what Job was feeling when he said:

If I am guilty—woe to me!
Even if I am innocent, I cannot lift my head,
for I am full of shame
and drowned in my affliction. (Job 10 v 15)

When our emotions are in turmoil, it's difficult to know who's responsible for what. We may fear we did the right thing for the wrong reason, or the wrong thing for the right reason, or maybe we did a lot of wrong things. Thankfully, God knows all. We can pray, as David did, for his help to untangle our Borrowed Guilt and our Legitimate Guilt— those things that are not our fault and that we should not feel guilty about, and those things that are our responsibility and that we are right to feel guilty over:

> *Search me, O God, and know my heart;*
> *Try me and know my anxious thoughts;*
> *And see if there be any hurtful way in me,*
> *And lead me in the everlasting way.*
>
> *(Psalm 139 v 23-24, NASB)*

OUR ABUSER'S GUILT

When Borrowed Guilt arises, we can say, "This isn't my fault. It was outside my control. My abuser owns their own sin." If we can't say that, or can't confidently feel that reality, we can ask God to ease our conscience.

Because I grew up in a Christian home, another question that plagued my mind was "Is my dad genuinely saved, or is he a wolf in sheep's clothing?" He said he was a Christian, but his actions often contradicted his words.

In the Psalms, David seems certain of his enemies' lack of salvation. He confidently asks God to judge violent men and rain disaster on the heads of his oppressors. But David had at least two advantages over me. First, David was a prophet who heard the voice of God. Second, in Old Testament times, Israel was the chosen people of God, and David was his chosen king over them. Persecuting Israel and opposing David was usually an expression of opposing God himself. David knew his enemies were God's enemies, and he wasn't sinning when he asked God to judge them.

For us, it's much harder to distinguish genuine believers from hypocrites. We can't see into people's hearts, and God rarely if ever reveals his will apart from the Bible. God's chosen people are now a spiritual family, not a clearly defined nation or demographic. Many who are now lost will be saved, and some who claim to love Jesus in truth do not.

Jesus warned:

> *Not everyone who says to me, "Lord, Lord" will enter the kingdom of heaven, but only the one who does the will of my Father who is in heaven. (Matthew 7 v 21)*

When someone claims to be a believer but stubbornly lives in unrepentant sin, we have legitimate reason to question their authenticity. If they're not exhibiting any fruits of the Spirit—love, joy, peace, patience, kindness, goodness, faithfulness, gentleness, and self-control (Galatians 5 v 22-23)—or showing any signs of remorse or change, we can ask God to either work in their hearts or reveal their true nature. We can be wise without condemning. We can be wary without being unhopeful. Or, we may feel as certain as David did, and plead with God to do his righteous will.

We can adapt David's prayers to our era, saying, "Lord, don't let their sin continue. If you're going to save them, save them quickly. If not, please stop them from continuing to commit evil."

We can entrust our abusive loved ones to our just and merciful God. He sees through every lie, straight into their heart of hearts. He has authority to judge and power to save. In Revelation 1 v 18, Jesus says, "I hold the keys of death and Hades."

But perhaps the idea of God's mercy concerns you. A young woman once asked me, "I'm afraid God might be too merciful. What if he forgives my abuser? What if I get to heaven, but can't feel safe or happy because he's there too?" Survivor, behold your God:

He will wipe every tear from their eyes. There will be no more death or mourning or crying or pain, for the old order of things has passed away.

(Revelation 21 v 4)

What is "the old order of things"?

Sin.

Brokenness.

Injustice.

Death.

Your abuser will not be in heaven because even if God saves them, your abuser will be your abuser no longer. They will be themselves, yet without any evil. It will be like meeting them, the "them" that is how God intended them to be, for the very first time.

And, if your abuser does not repent, God will justly judge and righteously condemn them. There is no statute of limitations in the courtroom of God. There is no parole, early release, or maximum length of sentencing in hell. It's an eternal and complete separation from God's love and God's people.

OUR GUILT

As survivors, we often fear God won't forgive us. We're so used to being unforgiven by an evil abuser that we can't imagine being forgiven by a holy God. But God is not abusive. In fact, one of God's primary characteristics is love, so much so that 1 John 4 v 8b-9 says...

God is love. This is how God showed his love among us: He sent his one and only Son into the world that we might live through him.

All people are sinners. Guilt is the right response to our sin. But there is a way to own our guilt, and then deal with it—or rather, have it dealt with by Another. Our sin, our guilt, and our pain don't need to define us. As Mike McKinley notes in his book *Passion*, it's helpful to analyze the actions of Judas, Peter, and the Pharisees, as Jesus stood on trial and was condemned to death. They were all sinners. Each had rejected the Son of God. All should have felt guilty, because they were.

The Pharisees puffed themselves up with their own good deeds. Instead of confronting their sin and accepting Jesus as the Messiah, they lashed out in blame-shifting, guilt-tripping, and lies. When Judas went to see them and confessed "I have sinned … for I have betrayed innocent blood," they responded, "What is that to us? … That's your responsibility" (Matthew 27 v 4). They shifted their guilt onto Judas, heaping Borrowed Guilt on top of his own Legitimate Guilt.

Then there is Judas. In shame, he returned the blood money he was paid in exchange for disclosing Jesus' whereabouts. While making amends is good, it doesn't negate the reality of our sin. All our good deeds are but a dirty band-aid on the gaping stab-wound of our sinful nature. Having allowed his guilt to devour his hope, Judas killed himself in despair rather than seek Christ and repent. He hanged himself on a tree for sinning against the Savior who was hanged on a tree to give sinners new life.

By God's grace, we don't have to be like the Pharisees or Judas. We can follow Peter, who "wept bitterly" (Luke 22 v 62) when he realized he'd sinned by denying three times that he knew Jesus. He owned his Legitimate Guilt. But, as McKinley points out:

> "He didn't just weep. You can tell that he repented for his sins because his life changed after that moment. He was the first disciple to enter the empty tomb. After Jesus' resurrection from the dead, Peter was

> *reconciled to Him and received forgiveness from*
> *Him, just as Jesus had predicted (Luke 22 v 32)."*
> *(Passion, page 36)*

As Peter put it later in his life, Jesus "suffered once for sins, the righteous for the unrighteous, to bring you to God" (1 Peter 3 v 18). Like Peter, we can allow our guilt to drive us to repent—to drive us to the foot of the cross. We can gratefully allow God's Spirit to work in our hearts, changing our lives and behavior for the better. It's through Christ we can be rid of our deathly guilt, for he rose from death so we could rise too.

Don't project your abuser's guilt-tripping lies onto a God who is merciful and ready to forgive. Does the God who offers free forgiveness to all who repent match the god-you-imagine who finds you unforgivable no matter how you plead? Does the Messiah who said, "Come to me, all you who are weary and burdened, and I will give you rest" (Matthew 11 v 28) match the god-in-your-head who says you don't deserve to be loved? Does the God of the Bible who says, *Yes, you're a sinner, but I've paid the price for you,* match the god-in-your-head who brings up past offenses out of spite?

The god-in-your-head is a lie: a scarecrow constructed by Satan and your abuser's lies. The true God does not want you to be burdened by Borrowed Guilt, and he offers to remove your Legitimate Guilt.

God's forgiveness is greater, more powerful, and more permanent than any sin you could ever dream of committing. His love is powerful enough to wash away the guilt of murderers like King David, violent men like the apostle Paul, a demon-possessed woman like Mary Magdalene, and a prostitute like Rahab. Surely, if he can forgive these, he can wipe away every tear from your eye, and every fear from your soul, and fill you with assurance of his love.

PRAYER

Lord, forgive me for my sins. Take away my guilt and shame. Grant me the humility to see my own sin, the courage to discern other people's sin, and the wisdom to turn to you for mercy and absolution. Fill me with peace and an unshakable knowledge that you have forgiven me and you love me.

7. #WHYIDIDNTREPORT

Anyone who says, "Just leave,"
Has never felt the fear
Or that bitter agony
When you realize he will never be
The man that he could be.
He loved me and he couldn't stand me too
So I said, "Father, forgive me,
For you know not what you do."

For 400 years, the Israelites—God's people—were enslaved in Egypt. In an attempt to control population growth, Pharaoh forced them to live in poverty as he worked them to the bone. Nevertheless, their numbers continued to grow—and so Pharaoh ordered that all the baby boys should be murdered.

Having seen the affliction and heard the cries of his people, God sent Moses to emancipate them. But when Moses brought this good news to the Israelites, "They did not listen to Moses, because of their broken spirit and harsh slavery" (Exodus 6 v 9, ESV).

Because of their broken spirit. Abuse victims are often not unlike those enslaved Hebrews of old. Beaten down and broken in spirit, we're accustomed to oppression and we're acquainted with grief. Sometimes, when God opens an escape route in our lives, we shrink back in disbelief and fear.

It took me over a decade to report my abuse. My mom witnessed some of it, and though she was upset, she never told anyone, so for a long time I assumed either our situation was normal or nothing could be done about it. I tried to tell pastors and family friends, but as a child I didn't have the vocabulary to express what was wrong. When I said things like, "My dad has anger problems," nobody asked, "What do you mean?"

Why didn't I report? It's a question that many people who aren't survivors—and, I think, many who are—ask. Why do so many abuse victims wait years to report, if they ever do at all? Here's why.

THE LIES THEY TELL

Any time we buck an abuser's control we know we'll meet resistance. If we try to leave then, like Pharaoh, they'll manipulate, threaten, and lie. My dad used to say, "If anything ever happens to me, you guys will be living under a bridge." Looking back, that's ridiculous, because our church and friends would have taken care of us. At the time, though, it was a terrifying prospect.

I was made to feel guilty for not appreciating my dad's harassment. I was told he found me attractive because I resembled my mom. To complain would be ungrateful, and insult her. When my parents fought, I was made to feel responsible. I'd been asked to give them marital counseling, and was even told details of their sex lives. Was it their fault my advice hadn't worked? Would reporting them be a betrayal of confidence?

One of the hardest things for me to reconcile, as a Christian, was my longing to obey God while also protecting myself. If an abuser is religious, they often weaponize Scripture against their victim. They demand forgiveness, accuse them of sin, or claim God endorses their behavior.

I was taught I must keep forgiving my abuser no matter what. In our family, "Forgive me," was code for "Suck it up. Don't act crazy. Keep my secrets. Pretend this never happened."

Many people, including pastors, demanded that I follow the command, "Honor your father and your mother" (Exodus 20 v 12) in an unbiblical way. I was to stay quiet and submit to people who didn't submit to God. But this is a dangerous twisting of Scripture, and not what the command means at all.

Ephesians 6 v 1-4 tells us:

> *Children, obey your parents in the Lord, for this is right. "Honor your father and mother"—which is the first commandment with a promise—"so that it may go well with you and that you may enjoy long life on the earth." Fathers, do not exasperate your children; instead, bring them up in the training and instruction of the Lord.*

Note that it says, "Children, obey your parents *in the Lord*." If a parent says or does something in opposition to the Lord, the child is not required to comply. For example, if a child is told by his mom to lie, then his obedience to God, who tells us not to lie, supersedes his obedience to his mom. To honor someone means to treat them with honesty, fairness, and integrity. We honor others by being honorable ourselves. We do not honor them by pretending they're honorable even if they're not. We hold them accountable for their actions, reject dishonorable behavior, and minimize their ability to treat us dishonorably.

Our longing to overlook a parent's faults is natural. Sadly, sometimes the only way we can honor them is by loving them enough to stand up to them, and refusing to serve as an outlet for their cruelty, anger, and lust. We honor them by not allowing them to pretend abuse is OK. If our trust, compassion, obedience, or relationship are a means through which they express evil, we can, biblically, refuse to "walk in step with the wicked or stand in the way that sinners take or sit in the company of mockers" (Psalm 1 v 1).

Paul's letter to the Romans tells Christians, "If possible, so far as it depends on you, live peaceably with all" (Romans 12 v 18, ESV). If possible. Sometimes, although we do our best to live peaceably with a parent, they continue to be disruptive and hostile. Ultimately, we honor God as our true Father.

Of course, as a teenager (let alone a young child) I wasn't able to work these things out on my own. All I heard at home was that I should forgive, forget, and obey.

So I did.

WHAT HOLDS US BACK

Another thing that holds us back from reporting is our own emotional confusion and stunned disbelief. We wish things were different. We hope they can change. Though we've been disappointed more times than we can count, we wonder if one last try could make the difference. We fear them and love them, miss them and want to escape them. We also don't trust the police, church, court system, or anyone else to truly keep us safe or restore our wholeness.

One of the most shocking stories in the Bible is when Tamar, King David's daughter, is raped by her brother Amnon. Absalom, her brother, wanted revenge. David, her father, wanted to sweep it under the rug. Only God told the truth, and his testimony on behalf of Tamar endures to this day.

When Absalom found his sister, Tamar, she was weeping inconsolably, her royal robes torn. Immediately, he knew she'd been raped. "Has that Amnon, your brother, been with you?" he asked. "Be quiet for now, my sister; he is your brother. Don't take this thing to heart" (2 Samuel 13 v 20).

Instead of confronting Amnon, Absalom encouraged his sister to stay quiet, and he himself stayed quiet too. "And Tamar lived in her brother Absalom's house, a desolate woman."

When their father, King David, heard what Amnon had done, "he was furious" (v 21). But it's what we're *not* told that speaks volumes. David did nothing to give Tamar justice. Instead, he stayed quiet too.

For two long years, Absalom nourished hatred in his heart: hatred for his rapist brother and hatred for his neglectful father. Eventually, Absalom hatched a plan. He lured Amnon to a party in the fields. As the brothers drank wine and sheared Absalom's sheep, he signaled to his servants, who slaughtered Amnon like an animal in the pastures (2 Samuel 13 v 23-29).

Again, David was upset. He mourned his son, Amnon, despite him having raped Tamar. Again, David did nothing. Evil was allowed to fester for another three years.

Steeped in bitterness, Absalom conspired against his father. He employed his charm and skills in manipulation to win Israel over to himself. So great was his hold over the people that David fled in fear for his life.

War ensued, and during the battle Absalom was slain. The brother who loved his sister, but encouraged her to stay quiet, made himself a murderer and died violently. The father who was furious over his daughter's victimization, yet did nothing, lost two sons.

In 2 Samuel 18 v 32-33, David learned of Absalom's death and mourned his son. It's easy to imagine David weeping and wishing he had died instead. Perhaps he was recalling all the things he could have done differently.

But Joab, the commander of Israel's armies, was offended, saying, "You love those who hate you and hate those who love you" (19 v 6).

Joab was right. David loved his evil sons more than the soldiers who risked their lives to defend him. More even than his daughter, whom he failed to defend or bring justice for.

Only one person reported Tamar's rape, and that was God. He recorded it in his book for all of time, so that nearly 3,000 years later we could feel her betrayal.

I can relate to Tamar in this story. I know what it's like to have everyone you trust let you down. I can even relate to Absalom. I know how heart-wrenching it is to have a parent disappoint you so profoundly.

And I can relate to David—because I know what it's like to love an abuser. We blind ourselves in denial. We want to bend over backwards to save them from themselves. "Just a little more patience, and maybe they'll become patient; a little more love, and hopefully they'll grow loving; a little more prayer, and maybe they'll repent and change."

Like David, I was desperate to love a man overcome by hate. I wanted to pretend abuse had never happened. When people at church questioned my dad's character, I was angry. "How dare they think my dad could be unsaved? How dare they rile him up? Don't they understand the delicate situation we're in? If he could just get some friends, some good men who'd inspire him to be good too, everything would be fine." But it wasn't.

FEAR OF REVENGE

"Did you hear that story on the news today? A man came home and caught his wife and kids trying to leave. He shot them all dead, then killed himself. You better never try to leave me."

It was made clear to me that, if I ever tried to leave or speak out, something terrible would happen. I'd seen what his gun could do to a dog. I'd seen his capacity for rage and violence. One day, while he was at work and my mom was distracted, I snuck into his room. I removed the gun from its case, and put the case back on the shelf. I prayed he wouldn't notice it was empty. I made sure the gun wasn't loaded, and folded it into a towel. Then I carried it downstairs and hid it in my closet at the bottom of a box of craft supplies.

That evening, my stomach churned as he entered his room. I tried to keep myself busy, to avoid wondering what would happen if he noticed. After a while he came out. He stood there, stoic, staring at me. But then went about his regular routine. He pretended nothing was wrong, but I knew he knew.

Did you hear that story on the news today? Every day, victims die. Every day, evil people commit unspeakable atrocities against their own families. Even now I have night-mares. I keep my cell phone on-hand in case something terrible happens. Our home alarm system is always on. It's been 13 years, and still I do not know how to not be afraid.

FEAR OF BEING DISBELIEVED

None of the adults in my childhood who witnessed me being abused reported it. None of the friends or pastors I dropped hints to asked questions or seemed concerned. When I finally reported as an adult, friends, strangers, and relatives questioned my sanity. I was called an attention-seeker and mentally unstable. One relative compared me to Potiphar's wife, the manipulative woman in Genesis 39 who tried to seduce Joseph and who, when she failed, false-ly accused him of rape and had him imprisoned. Rather than compare me to Tamar, I was compared to the worst kind of liar.

Remarks such as "What were you wearing?" and "What did you do to make him act like that?" are thrown regularly at survivors who report. We could be compared to people in the Bible such as Dinah, who was raped and later avenged; Esther, who led her people despite being objectified; or Jonathan, who defied his abusive father and protected his friend. But no. Instead, we often get compared to the one woman in the entire Bible who made false accusations against a godly man—and for me, the comparison was made by a loved one who knew exactly what I'd endured.

Jesus' family thought he was crazy because of his claims about himself (Mark 3 v 21). He knows what it's like to be disbelieved. So do too many survivors who report. When we begin telling our story and the truth about who we are as survivors, our loved ones are often the first to disbelieve or slander. Sometimes, those we should be able to trust the most—people who witnessed our victimization or perhaps were fellow victims themselves—turn against us.

So, it's easy to understand why this fear of being disbelieved—this fear that our family can't handle our pain—often makes us hesitate to report. However, no relationship can remain healthy when such life-altering secrets are suppressed. We must love those close to us enough to trust them and give them the chance to weep with us if they will. When I told a dear friend and pastor's wife that I'd been compared to Potiphar's wife, she said, "No, that's Satan talking. You're like Paul. You've suffered immense pain, but you use that pain to honor God." That was one of the kindest things anyone has ever said to me.

FEAR OF BEING BELIEVED

When I was a child, I feared being believed. I feared my parents getting divorced. I feared being taken by Child Protective

Services and separated from my sisters. I thought my silence would hold my family together.

As a teenager, I hesitated to tell my mom because I believed it would break her heart. After all the tumult she'd been through, I didn't think she could handle one more trauma. Sometimes the truth is so terrible that telling it is risky.

When I finally did report, it was difficult to look the police in the eye because I felt their pity. Seeing seasoned officers express sorrow and shock made me realize to a new degree how bad things had been.

After publicly telling the truth, I was faced with embarrassing questions, unsolicited advice, and gossip. I felt emotionally naked, as if every private pain and humiliation was on display. Strangers were examining and picking over my stories the way grocery shoppers pick over produce. I wanted pity, yet I hated pity. I wanted truth but was stung by the cold chill of exposure. Looking back, I'm glad I shared the truth, because it was a major milestone in my recovery process. Strange as it may seem, being believed is not easy. It means your abuser is an abuser. It means you are a victim. It means all your pain is real.

FEAR OF WORLDLY JUSTICE

If you've ever served on a jury, you know how stark a courtroom can feel. People's private lives are laid bare. Evidence is exhibited like slabs of meat at a butcher's shop. Victims and witnesses are trotted out like show animals, asked personal questions, and pour out their pain to an impersonal room. A stenographer clacks down transcripts and lawyers gesticulate, reducing years of immeasurable suffering into an hour-glass. Your most intimate injuries become pawns on a chess board.

These worldly courts are imperfect. As much as we want to believe we can right wrongs and give victims justice, we can only offer fragmented peace and a dehumanizing legal process. Unfortunately, if we hang all our hope of recovery and peace on earthly justice, we may find it falls short of the closure we crave. The reason why we report and seek prosecution cannot be the hope of wholeness. Even if our abuser is convicted, our pain will still be with us, and nothing can rewind time or undo history.

FEAR OF NO JUSTICE

Linked to this, of course, is the fear that we'll endure all that humiliating agony for nothing. What if we are brave and file that police report, but law enforcement decides there's not enough evidence to prosecute? What if they do prosecute, we endure a lengthy trial, and our abuser gets a "not guilty" verdict?

And it never goes away, this fear. On September 13, 2018, over 16 years after she was abducted, Elizabeth Smart pleaded with Utah authorities to reconsider releasing Wanda Barzee, the woman who assisted in her kidnapping. On June 5, 2002, when Elizabeth was 14, she was dragged from her bedroom at knifepoint and held captive for nine months. During that time, she was raped repeatedly. The release of a convicted criminal, years sooner than expected, shocked and terrified Elizabeth.

Such miscarriages of justice strike fear into the hearts of many who are considering reporting. We fear living in a world where the dangerous people we have accused roam free; we fear being unprotected from abusers who know we told on them.

LONGING TO GO BACK

It wasn't until the Israelites saw the mighty hand of the Lord displayed against the Egyptians that they feared the Lord and trusted him to save. After they escaped, and were journeying toward their new home in the promised land, they began to doubt God's plan. The road was long and hard, fraught with difficulties, and filled with uncertainty.

"If only we had died by the Lord's hand in Egypt!" the Israelites complained in Exodus 16 v 3:

> *There we ... ate all the food we wanted, but you have brought us out into this desert to starve this entire assembly to death.*

Notice how they idealize their slavery. They recall fine dining and being provided for, but we know they were deprived and persecuted until their spirit was broken. Their baby boys were murdered, yet they manage to romanticize the experience of pain that they are used to.

Sometimes coming out of a bad situation feels like jumping out of the frying pan into the fire. In our abuser's house we had a roof over our heads. We had rules, albeit harsh ones, that gave structure and a sense of living up to a standard. However dysfunctional our home, we knew our place in it. Once we break free, like those slaves unused to freedom from Egypt, we feel out of our element. Was it really that bad? Is this overwhelming new reality really any better?

We are refugees fleeing oppression, exiles from broken homes and sin. Don't long for the darkness behind you. Instead, look ahead. The Egypt where you were provided for is a mirage. The love of your abuser is an illusion.

Eventually, I realized I had two dads. I had the man who made me feel like prey, and the man I dreamed would someday protect me. I had the dad who got angry and said terrible things, and the one who studied theology and I could imagine being godly. One day I realized the dad I hoped for had died. The things I loved about him—his intelligence, curiosity, and passion for grappling with doctrinal truth—

had passed away. Maybe the dad I hoped for had never existed at all. I don't know.

WHY I DID REPORT

Into Your hand I commit my spirit;
You have ransomed me, O LORD, God of truth.
(Psalm 31 v 5, NASB)

Even after I escaped my dad's control, I didn't report. It took me years to acknowledge what had happened to me. I knew I was heartbroken. I knew I felt defiled. But I saw so many horror stories on the news and compared myself to those victims. By comparison, yes, my suffering was minor, but those stories were the worst of the worst. In the end, it wasn't stories of other survivors that unblinded me though. It was the love of my husband, who was so unlike my dad.

Eventually, my parents divorced. I told myself the courts must have all the information they needed to prosecute if they could. When nothing happened, I was taken aback. I assumed the police were powerless to help.

I knew I'd been abused, but didn't want to accept that dad was evil. I didn't want to believe God would let something so horrible consume someone I loved. Ironically, it was my dad who cleared things up for me.

"I don't know what to think," I told him one day, over the phone. "I can either believe you're crazy and didn't know what you were doing, or you're evil and understood completely."

I understood from what he said in reply that he did not feel he was crazy, and so I was going to have to accept that he was evil.

That was the last time I spoke to him.

While earthly justice is finite, and maybe unattainable, we can find peace knowing we've reported the truth and done everything in our power to empower other victims. Confronting the sin of an abuser is not dishonoring, but loving. How can they otherwise repent of sins which they themselves deny? If our abuser is to have any hope of salvation, or of normal, healthy human happiness, we will help them by calling their sin what it is.

When we confront sin, we reflect the truthfulness of Jesus himself. In John 4, he minces no words when calling the Samaritan woman to repent of adultery. In Matthew 23, Jesus publicly labels the religious leaders of his day bloodthirsty hypocrites (e.g. v 13, 15, 23) and a brood of vipers (v 33). Though telling the truth is often daunting, we can rely upon Jesus for strength and ultimate vindication. Our God does not ignore sin or pretend it never happened. Rather, he brings it to our attention, calls it what it is, and calls us to repent.

I've come to accept I won't find justice in this life. Much of my abuse was experienced long ago. The bruises have healed. Any evidence there was is gone. People who witnessed it never reported. Even if a case was made, could I find comfort in my dad's sentencing? For a while I was angry. Then I realized my anger was only prolonging my suffering.

I've reported what I can to law enforcement. Should any additional victims come forward, my testimony will bolster theirs. I feel confident I've done everything I can to protect others, but I'm not anxious for worldly justice. I cannot pin my heart on a hope so unlikely and imperfect. Instead, I find peace knowing God is just. He has all the evidence he needs, because he was there.

In Luke 12 v 2-3, Jesus says:

There is nothing concealed that will not be disclosed, or hidden that will not be made known. What you have said in the dark will be heard in the daylight,

> *and what you have whispered in the ear in the inner*
> *rooms will be proclaimed from the roofs.*

God is my witness and attorney. He's my abuser's prosecutor and judge. He makes no mistakes.

I find great peace knowing justice will one day be served by divine authority. That truth is what enabled me to report the truth to human authorities. I can endure the prospect of folly and ignorance and accusation now, because my Father knows the inner heart of every abuser. He knows my testimony is true, and remembers far more wrongs than I do. The unrepentant abuser's tiniest and most secret offense will be brought to light and justice in God's courtroom.

In Luke 12 v 4-5, Jesus continues:

> *I tell you, my friends, do not be afraid of those who*
> *kill the body and after that can do no more. But I*
> *will show you whom you should fear: Fear him who,*
> *after your body has been killed, has authority to*
> *throw you into hell. Yes, I tell you, fear him.*

God's courtroom is the zenith of perfect justice. He is utterly holy. For those who lived at enmity with him, it's a place of condemnation and dread. The greater the evil someone commits in this life, the more harrowing their day in God's courtroom will be. Their punishment, as they're cast from God's presence, will fit their crimes more than we can understand.

THE ULTIMATE DIVIDING LINE

But we mustn't make the mistake of thinking the ultimate dividing line of God's justice is between victims and abusers. It's between those who love Jesus and those who reject his salvation:

*Then I saw a great white throne and him who was
seated on it. The earth and the heavens fled from his
presence, and there was no place for them. And I saw
the dead, great and small, standing before the throne,
and books were opened. Another book was opened,
which is the book of life. The dead were judged
according to what they had done as recorded in the
books. The sea gave up the dead that were in it, and
death and Hades gave up the dead that were in them,
and each person was judged according to what they
had done. (Revelation 20 v 11-13)*

Think about this for a moment. There are books in eternity
with your name in them. Sailors who drowned at sea will be
raised and held accountable for either their actions or the
actions of Jesus. Ashes will be gathered, dust reformed, and
men and women from millennia past will have their lives
remembered: either their sins tallied or their faith validated.

If we stand before God on the basis of our own merit,
we'll be rightly excluded from his perfect presence. But there
is a "book of life," containing the names of those who have
asked Jesus to forgive them, who have been credited with his
perfection. And Jesus promises:

*I will never blot out the name of that person from the
book of life, but will acknowledge that name before
my Father and his angels. (Revelation 3 v 5)*

If you are a survivor, whether you report or not—now or in
twenty years—is a personal decision you alone can make,
but one that is very important. Sometimes, it's right to
report abuse. Maybe we're protecting ourselves. Maybe we're
staunching a loved one's flow of sin. Maybe we're protecting other people from becoming victims. Maybe, in order

to heal, we simply need to document the truth. Sometimes, the abuse we endure—while evil and traumatizing—is un-recognized as a crime by finite worldly courts. Regardless, we can take comfort knowing a report has been filed in the courtroom of God. For just as God remembered Tamar, so God remembers us, for all of time. He will grant justice. He will not forget.

So I have put my hope in this God: the God who...

> made heaven and earth,
>   the sea, and all that is in them,
> who keeps faith forever;
>   who executes justice for the oppressed,
>   who gives food to the hungry.
> The LORD sets the prisoners free;
>   the LORD opens the eyes of the blind.
> The LORD lifts up those who are bowed down;
>   the LORD loves the righteous.
> The LORD watches over the sojourners;
>   he upholds the widow and the fatherless,
>   but the way of the wicked he brings to ruin.
>   (Psalm 146 v 6-9, ESV)

8. UNEARTHING THE IMAGE OF GOD

Often, as I write to you, I feel I'm on an archaeological dig inside my mind. I excavate pain, dust it off, analyze it, and catalog it in my collection. The process is sobering when it comes to old memories, but for more recent traumas and newer pains, it becomes less like archaeology and more like digging shrapnel out of a wound.

When a friend asked me to write this chapter—about how as humans we're innately valuable, created in the image of God—I thought, "Sure! That will be easy." After all, I've heard this since childhood, and western culture is soaked in this concept, insofar as equality is an ideal, human rights is part of our language, and all people—regardless of ethnicity, religion, or gender—are held to be valuable.

But the more I wrote, the more I realized I don't believe this about myself. In fact, writing this chapter has developed into a full-scale mining expedition to unearth the image of God in me: to prove to myself I am who I am, so I can show you your value too.

I know, in my head, I am made in God's image. It isn't something we earn, nor anything we can lose. It's imprinted in our intellect, our human characteristics, our very nature.

The Bible often compares God to a potter (for instance, Romans 9 v 21). I imagine him sculpting and forming our souls from clay, leaving behind his fingerprints: proof of his identity. No one can justifiably deny our legitimacy or importance, our value or dignity. Yet I struggle to feel this for myself in my heart.

I know, in my head, that our *Imago Dei*—the image of God—is why we have language while animals remain dumb, why we create breathtaking art, develop technological and scientific breakthroughs, build kingdoms and nations, and strive to fulfill his command to rule and maintain the world. Whether we intend to or not, we mirror the God who speaks, invents, builds, and sustains.

I know all this in my head, yet I struggle to believe it in my heart.

It's difficult to feel confident in your value when you've been taught for years that you're inferior—when your thoughts and opinions have been treated as stupid, your feelings as irrational, your personality as a nuisance, and your body as an object to be lusted over or beaten up. Yet, if the unearthed fossil of a dinosaur's claw in clay is valuable and precious, how much more so the soul of one who bears the fingerprints of the Lord of the universe?

THE ORIGIN OF DIGNITY

As often happens in archaeology, in order to understand the treasure we're holding, we must go back in time and consider it in context. In this case, we must travel back to the creation of the world.

In the beginning, the Spirit of God hovered over the face of the waters (Genesis 1 v 1-2). The Son, who we know as Jesus, was also there (John 1 v 1-3). The Light of the world was present when the Father said, "Let there be light!" And so we can see that the Father, Son, and Holy Spirit were all present, working in harmony, at the dawn of time. Not created. Always existing. Equal in power and glory.

And, for the pinnacle of his creation, God said, "Let us make mankind in our image, in our likeness" (Genesis 1 v 26). God spoke to himself in the first person plural because he is three Persons: the Father, the Son, and the Spirit. He designed us to have creativity and innovation, delight and longing, curiosity and intelligence, just like him. He created us to reflect—to image—him to each other and the world, to rule over his earth under his guidance (Genesis 1 v 28-30; 2 v 15-17), and to relate to each other and him, just as he is relational himself. "For from him and through him and for him are all things. To him be the glory forever! Amen" (Romans 11 v 36).

There is a sacred facet to us, however buried in sin and tarnished by mortality it may be. We were intended to reflect God's love, joy, peace, patience, kindness, goodness, faithfulness, gentleness, self-control, and grace to everyone and all the world around us. We were made to enjoy him, and enjoy belonging to him.

FALLEN FROM GRACE

But then one day, in a beautiful garden called Eden, Adam and Eve disobeyed God. By rebelling against his rule, they didn't merely take a bite of forbidden fruit; they attempted to become like God (Genesis 3 v 5, 22). They wanted to define their own identity, on their own terms, apart from their Creator. Instead of enjoying being like God, they wanted to be equal with God. They bucked their divine-image-bearing nature, sending aftershocks of sin and death into future generations. Their reflection of God was left cracked, fragmented by sin—but God promised to send a redeemer (v 15).

After banishment from Eden, Adam and Eve turned back to God. They had two sons, Cain and Abel, whom they taught to worship God and pray. However, Cain's heart was not in it. While Abel brought God the best sacrifice he could, Cain offered what he could do without. The seed of his father's sin had taken root, and though he heard God's voice and was made in God's image, he did not love God. He worshiped begrudgingly, going through the motions, his heart elsewhere (4 v 3-5).

When God rejected Cain's hypocrisy, Cain grew angry. He felt entitled to God's approval and resented his brother's faith. God warned Cain:

> *Why are you angry? Why is your face downcast? If you do what is right, will you not be accepted? But if you do not do what is right, sin is crouching at your door; it desires to have you, but you must rule over it.*
> *(v 6-7)*

But Cain called to his brother Abel, saying, "Let's go out to the field." And as they walked through the fields, Cain's envy consumed him and he struck down his brother (v 8). "What have you done?" the Lord asked Cain. "Listen! Your brother's blood cries out to me from the ground" (v 10).

Like Cain, we are descendants of Adam. Riddled with deception, jealousy, greed, and pride, our *Imago Dei* is tarnished, at times almost indiscernible. We don't treat others with love or respect. We don't view ourselves in light of God's love. We don't remember our Creator.

AN IMAGE DEFACED

While our own sin tarnishes our image-bearing nature, abusers work to deface it even further. Whether they realize it or not, they strive to finish the rebellion Adam and Eve began, teaching us that our worth revolves around their moods and opinions; that we're worthless, shameful, disgusting, and unlovable; that we exist to serve them, and are meaningless outside of that twisted relationship.

It becomes even harder to accept that we are made in the image of God when, by extension, that means we must also accept that our abuser is too. How can we value someone whose behavior is worthless? How can we honor one who is dishonorable?

Most people, survivor or no, have been mocked, falsely accused, hurt, or betrayed. At one point or another, our suffering has been minimized, ignored, or ridiculed. For abuse survivors, this experience can be particularly personal. We may be accused of failing as a husband or wife, or asked what we did to catch a rapist's eye. This further buries our worth under the mud of shame and the muck of lies.

Even well-intentioned people sometimes don't know how to respond when we say we've been abused. I once confided in a church friend who stopped me, saying, "Let's not talk about that. That's what we have pastors for." All I wanted was for her to listen. All I wanted was for someone to be with me, to act as though it mattered—as though I mattered.

Satan and our disoriented consciences rub our noses in our shame. Our insecurities are bolstered by disbelieving glances and dismissive pats on the back. We're overwhelmed by diagnoses like PTSD, and our depression and anxiety are condemned as sin or "weak faith" by some. But David said in Psalm 109 v 22, "I am afflicted and needy, and my heart is wounded within me" (NASB)—clearly the greatest of God's servants suffer, and so only fools and liars condemn sorrow as sin.

Our image of God—our value and identity—becomes buried like an artifact beneath the dust of sin and death. We no longer perceive our worth or hear God's voice. Our dignity becomes an archaeological ruin, lost from view and long forgotten. We may start to feel like no one cares about our pain. We fear we're a drag to be around, "damaged goods," incapable of trust and deeper relationships.

I find it hard to believe I'm worth anything to God, so it becomes hard to believe I'm going to heaven too. I know in my head Christ died for me. He forgave my sins the instant I repented. But… seriously? Me? Can I be loved by a perfect God? Can I be forgiven by a glorious Creator? I'm not used to trusting love. I don't take acceptance for granted. I expect abandonment, tricks, and gaslighting, because that's what I'm used to.

BODY, HEART, MIND

Abuse is never only physical.

The cuts and the bruises may heal, but the wounds run deep, into our very souls. It's interesting to note that we ourselves, as humans, have something of a triune nature. The Bible sometimes notes that God created us with a body, heart, and mind. I've found it very helpful to think of myself as having these three basic categories: physical body, emotional heart, and intellectual mind.

When we talk to ourselves, the conversation tends to be between our emotional and intellectual selves, between our feelings and our logic, between what we desire and what we know is right. Meanwhile our bodies interject and influence the conversation with hormonal ups and downs, chemical changes, and the natural progression of mortality.

When trauma occurs, our body-heart-mind nature experiences intense inner conflict. Often sexual abuse victims feel aroused during victimization. That's because our bodies are physical mechanical creations. While our hearts may feel humiliated and our minds outraged, our bodies often simply respond to stimuli, similar to the way a computer responds to keystrokes or a vending machine responds to the right combination of change. So, an abuser who pushes the right buttons may elicit a predictable mechanical response from our bodies. Physical arousal during abuse creates huge and lasting guilt or shame, unfair and undeserved though those feelings are.

It's vital to recognize that while we're one person—one soul—what our bodies feel, our hearts desire, and our minds think can be (and often are) three separate and distinct things. It's how we process these emotions, thoughts, and sensations, and allow them to influence our spiritual health and real-world actions, that's ultimately important. Understanding our body-heart-mind nature can help us untangle what went on internally as we were abused externally. Being able to categorize our reactions according to body, heart, and mind helps us understand why we feel the things we feel, and puts our emotions in context.

While everyone's inner dialogue and thought processes will be different, it's easy to imagine what conflicts can occur. For instance, a rape victim could experience confusion similar to this:

- Body: *I am so attractive, I'm irresistible. While unexpected, this could be enjoyable.*
- Heart: *What? This is the worst thing that's ever happened to me! How can you feel aroused in any way? What's wrong with me? Make it stop! Make it stop!*
- Mind: *No! Lay low. If we don't struggle maybe it will end quickly and he won't hurt us too badly.*

A child who is being beaten might have another experience:

- Body: *When will the pain stop? It doesn't feel like it will ever stop!*
- Heart: *Why didn't I do a better job? He hates me because I failed. Look what I've done to him! He's so upset!*
- Mind: *This isn't my fault. He's a horrible person! I don't deserve this.*

A child who is molested may reason:

- Body: *This is strange. Something's not right. I don't understand.*
- Heart: *They must love me though, right? I'm making them happy. I'm being good. I trust them. It must be OK, right?*
- Mind: *Don't tell anyone. Something is wrong, but I don't understand. How can I hope to explain what I don't understand? What if I've done something bad?*

Three dimensions. Three reactions. One soul.

Understand, whatever inner conflict you feel is normal. You're not broken or insane for having conflicting emotions. The confusion you suffer—this cocktail of reactions and contradictory ideas—is no indication you're foolish, or weird, or without hope. Rather, this is the normal and understandable reaction of a complex person designed in the image of a complex God.

When God created humankind, his verdict was that "it was very good" (Genesis 1 v 31). Though this world is fallen and our nature corrupted by sin, our emotional blueprint is not intended to accommodate evil. You are processing a situation you were never designed to deal with in the first place.

As I look back, I remember logging onto my desktop and feeling curiosity and pleasure when I found my dad's pornography. That was my body talking. Then I looked through the doorway and saw my dad standing there, watching me, and I instantly felt fear and shame. That was my heart talking. Afterwards I grew angry, realizing he'd put the porn there on purpose and wanted to watch me find it. That was my mind talking. Body, heart, and mind, yet one soul, forever.

Is it any wonder that survivors struggle to see themselves as worthy of anything, or valuable in any way? Is it any wonder my heart has struggled to believe what my head knows to be true: that I'm made in the image of a wonderful God?

JESUS TAKES US PERSONALLY

When our already-fallen natures are afflicted by the evil of others and the trauma of abuse, it becomes harder than ever to trust the love of God. We want to believe we're valuable, but all we see are the cracks: the gaping holes between fragments of a treasure seemingly destroyed beyond hope or recognition.

Somewhere in a box, high on a closet shelf, is a picture frame bearing a dictionary-style definition of me:

> *Jennifer Michelle Greenberg:*
> *1: a human made in God's image, intrinsically*
> *valuable, a daughter of God, redeemed by Christ,*
> *bought with his blood, filled by his Spirit, because*
> *he loves her.*
> *2: a wife, mother, friend who is valued and loved.*

It takes knowing Jesus to restore our sense of dignity—to enable us to take that picture frame out, dust it off, and put it front and center.

For who establishes truth? Who has authority to say to me, "You are valuable," or "You're irredeemable?" Certainly not my abuser. Certainly not me. Even if the Pope or Billy Graham or the apostle Peter himself were to rate my worth, their opinion would mean nothing apart from God's.

The only one who can establish and validate my worth is Jesus. Just as we were made in the image of God, God became man, in the image of us. Despite being all-powerful and immortal, Jesus didn't consider heavenly glory something to cling to, but made himself lowly and was born into poverty, taking on the status of a servant (Philippians 2 v 6-8). The fact that Jesus came to earth at all gives us an idea of how valuable God considers his image-bearing creatures to be.

During his earthly life, Jesus treated others—the poor, the hurting, the broken, and the outcast—with a level of dignity that would be considered counter-cultural even in our progressive modern era. Thieves, prostitutes, lepers, and widows—he granted them honor though he himself was dishonored.

In Matthew 25 v 31-46, Jesus describes his future second coming. It's striking how strongly he relates to the weak, innocent, and helpless. In fact, he takes kindness to them so personally that it's as if the kindness was done directly to him. On that last day, Jesus says, he'll say to those who love him:

> *Come, you who are blessed by my Father; take your inheritance, the kingdom prepared for you since the creation of the world. For I was hungry and you gave me something to eat, I was thirsty and you gave me something to drink, I was a stranger and you invited me in, I needed clothes and you clothed me, I was sick and you looked after me, I was in prison and you came to visit me. (v 34-36)*

Then God's people will ask:

> *Lord, when did we see you hungry and feed you, or thirsty and give you something to drink? When did we see you a stranger and invite you in, or needing clothes and clothe you? When did we see you sick or in prison and go to visit you? (v 37-39)*

And he'll reply:

> *Truly I tell you, whatever you did for one of the least of these brothers and sisters of mine, you did for me.*
> *(v 40)*

By contrast, Jesus takes the neglect and harm of his children so seriously that it's as if those wrongs were committed personally against him.

Jesus will tell the wicked:

> *Depart from me, you who are cursed, into the eternal fire prepared for the devil and his angels. For I was hungry and you gave me nothing to eat, I was thirsty and you gave me nothing to drink, I was a stranger and you did not invite me in, I needed clothes and you did not clothe me, I was sick and in prison and you did not look after me. (v 41-43)*

They'll also ask:

> *Lord, when did we see you hungry or thirsty or a stranger or needing clothes or sick or in prison, and did not help you? (v 44)*

He will reply:

> *Truly I tell you, whatever you did not do for one of the least of these, you did not do for me. (v 45)*

Jesus identifies so closely with us that it's as if every hurtful word was aimed at him—every slap, slander, or instance of neglect was done directly to him. Everything my dad did to me, he may as well have done to Christ himself.

But Jesus takes his empathy with us even further, because he was willing to be tried, tortured, and executed in our stead, so we could be freed from enmity with God and restored to relationship with our Creator. This is how much God loves his children.

Being fully God and fully man simultaneously, Jesus' perfect life was priceless. If you added up all the offerings ever sacrificed, all the praises ever prayed, and all the good deeds done between creation and the end of time, they wouldn't be worth one fraction of a drop of his blood. Anytime I fear God doesn't think I'm valuable, I need to remember: he thinks that I am worth suffering for and that I am worth dying for.

His death was such a profound shock to the universe that the very earth trembled, the sky went black, and some who were dead came back to life. It was as if creation itself shuddered in horror and amazement. No doubt Satan gloated, thinking he'd won, but imagine his shock when Jesus' tomb rolled open. The God who created life can't be bound by mortality. His power to defy death proves he has authority to resurrect us too. And he will not abandon us. He is faithful.

In one of his most famous parables, Jesus explained his love for us like this:

> Suppose one of you has a hundred sheep and loses one of them. Doesn't he leave the ninety-nine in the open country and go after the lost sheep until he finds it? And when he finds it, he joyfully puts it on his shoulders and goes home. Then he calls his friends and neighbors together and says, "Rejoice with me; I have found my lost sheep." (Luke 15 v 4-6)

The Lord Jesus promises in the Gospel of John that he sends his Spirit—that same Spirit who was there at the dawn of creation—to dwell in those who trust him, and "to be with [them] forever" (John 14 v 16). Not just today. Not just until you mess up again. Not just so long as you feel happy or hopeful. Forever.

My *Imago Dei*, that intrinsic image of God, is restored to former glory as I place my hope in Jesus. Though I may stray like a wandering sheep, the Spirit will draw me again and again into the forgiving arms of Jesus, until the day I step foot in heaven. In that promised land there will be no more fear, for God's work in me will be finished.

FUMBLING TOWARD HEAVEN

Meanwhile, here on earth, I struggle. I want to hurry up and recover—put all this messy pain behind me. I want to prove to myself and everyone that I've got all my ducks in a row. But these confusing emotions and self-doubts quickly backfire. I feel foolish, vulnerable, and inferior for having them. "Normal people aren't like this," I think. "A strong person wouldn't be so insecure."

We all have a tendency to worship something other than God: to find our sense of self and value in finite things. Our bodies are temples where we worship fitness, money, sex, power, intellect, technology, pastors, and celebrities. We burn our energy like incense, sacrifice our time like an offering, and strive to be the image-bearers of false gods such as pop culture, political movements, or our favorite sports team.

Jesus shows us our value isn't measured by a paycheck, how many friends we have, what we wear, our medical diagnosis, how others treat us, or even by the things we've done or not done. Our value is measured in Jesus. When we place our faith in him, his righteous life is credited to us. His Spirit pours into our hearts. Just as a tree grows towards the sun, we begin to grow toward the Light of the world. We begin to grow more like him, unearthing the image of God in us—reflecting him, ruling under him, relating to him.

While manipulation and mind games are what I'm used to, God doesn't gaslight, and God doesn't lie. He gave me my faith, and he is my value. I know I'm going to heaven, not because I've got a warm fuzzy feeling about it but because

God's Spirit works faith in me, and he is faithful and mighty to save. Faith, then, is not an emotion but a promise given to me by the One who is faithful and true.

In the beginning, God said, "Let there be light!" and light exploded across the universe. God's first recorded words stabbed through earth's darkness. Now the Light of the world, Jesus, tears through my spiritual darkness. His light shines in the darkness to this day, and the darkness cannot overcome it (John 1 v 1-5). Just as the Spirit moved over that primordial chaos at the dawn of time, so the Spirit is sovereign and moving through the chaos in my soul.

This Genesis of me is a lifelong process. Like the reseeding of Eden in my heart, God is lovingly and methodically undoing the spiritual damage of sin to make his new creation. "Therefore, if anyone is in Christ, the new creation has come: The old has gone, the new is here!" (2 Corinthians 5 v 17).

Someday, God will again create, proclaiming, "I am making everything new!" (Revelation 21 v 5). Then the Light of the world, Jesus Christ, will blaze through the darkness of this earth. Every eye will see him as truth explodes across the universe. He will wash away sin, sorrow, and death forever. The Light will shine in the darkness, and the darkness will vanish. He will gather his daughter into his presence. I'll be healed and made whole again. There will be no more tears or fears. My body, heart, and mind will be perfect, as if sin had never dared come near me at all.

And the God of all grace, who called you to
his eternal glory in Christ, after you have
suffered a little while, will himself restore you
and make you strong, firm and steadfast.
(1 Peter 5 v 10)

9. THE STRANGER INSIDE

Repressed in my heart of hearts;
But every so often he breaks the surface,
Possessing my coldest parts,
His deeds are mine and my cruel intentions;
A glimmer in the eye, I catch there in the mirror,
Behind my smiling face a dead man hides.

Everyone has a Stranger Inside: a cruel voice that mocks, lies to, and diminishes us.

One of my friends calls his "The Man in The Basement." He keeps that man bound, gagged, and hidden away, but every so often it breaks free to torment him. Most people—including those who've never experienced trauma—have this inner-mental bully, but for many survivors the Stranger has grown, garnered strength, and become louder and more venomous. Fueled by disturbing memories and our abuser's cruel words, it gives a booming voice to our insecurities and fears.

Sometimes when I'm struggling to accomplish goals, the Stranger echoes a rude high-school sports coach, sneering, "Are you even trying?" Other times, I'll be enjoying a nice dinner out with Jason, and it whispers, "Are you really going to eat that much?"

It tells me I'm a fraud: that eventually I'll fail, and everyone will realize how inferior, unqualified, and stupid I am. It tells me that Jason could do better, that I'm a subpar mother, and that, if something ever happened to me, my family would be just fine. At first, I tried to pretend the voice didn't exist. I hoped that if I ignored it, it would eventually go away. Unfortunately, this backfired. The more I ignored it, the louder and more savage the Stranger became. It was as if not acknowledging it made it angrier.

It wasn't until that evening in the kitchen though—that night when my husband was washing dishes and all my fears of abandonment rose to the surface—that I realized the Stranger inside sounded exactly like my dad.

While my bruises and injuries healed long ago, it's the backhanded compliments, lies, and cruel insinuations of spiritual, emotional, and psychological abuse which have poisoned me for decades. These are the things the Stranger echoes in my mind. Little insults, like muttering that I need to lose weight as I show off a new dress, saying my body looks slutty, or criticizing the way I smile; these things sound like something a middle-school bully or internet troll would say, but when they come from a parental figure or loved one, they're much harder to dismiss. They echo in your mind indefinitely.

The Stranger picks up insults the way a lint roller picks up lint. It then spits them back at you when you're tired, sad, or stressed, to maximize impact. Like leftover lasagna, insults have more flavor the second time around. When the Stranger runs out of insults to recycle, it twists benign remarks into barbs and suggests compliments could be lies.

Sometimes, we get so used to our abuser's cruel words that we begin to view everything through a lens of pain. Petty insults become devastating blows. Thoughtless comments are like surprisingly stinging paper-cuts.

Questions like "Are you wearing that to the party?" turn into "You look horrible." "When will dinner be done?" turns into "Why can't you get your act together?" "Why did you let the kids eat cookies on the couch?" is translated as "Did you even watch the children today—don't you care about them?" Innocent remarks intended at face value are interpreted as passive-aggressive insinuations that you're a complete failure as a human being. We begin second-guessing and distrusting the intent of good people who love us.

Hate is what we're used to. Manipulation is what we're accustomed to. Thus, our default is to assume spite and guile rather than tactlessness and innocence. We don't expect to be loved, and this can throw a wrench into our relationships with nice people.

FIND THE SOURCE

When I first realized the Stranger Inside sounded like my dad, I was terrified. It felt like he was still controlling me: as if a ghost was haunting me or I was losing my mind. He seemed to have the ability to interfere in my marriage, interrupt my thoughts, and insert himself into every situation.

As much as our abusers may wish it, they don't have power to possess our minds or infiltrate our thoughts. The Stranger is me. Your Stranger is you. They've injured us severely, and their cruelty still affects us, but our abusers are just people.

I was taught from a young age to have certain ingrained fears, insecurities, and vulnerabilities. Most victims, young and old, experience such a process incorporating tactics like manipulation, gaslighting, intimidation, and blame-shifting. This is how we were taught to think. But we can unlearn the lies. What our abusers could do externally, we can reverse internally. We can hack our brains, unravel the logic, counteract the insults, and replace hate with grace.

The first step in silencing the Stranger is to listen. I reminded myself, "Jenn, this is your mind expressing insecurities and vulnerabilities in a defensive manner." In light of this, the Stranger becomes a powerful tool against itself. It reveals our inner fears and highlights the damage causing our most acute pain.

Once I realized the Stranger would be critical no matter what, I stopped taking its words personally. I began listening to the insults, and then backtracking to their point of origin, so that I could find the patterns in the lies and start to develop counter arguments.

SATAN, THE ACCUSER

While the Stranger isn't a real being, its voice may imitate the lies of a very real being—the devil. If it echoes the words of a spiritual abuser, or tells us that God won't accept us, it can be very dangerous indeed. When confronted by the spiritual abusers of his day, Jesus said, "You belong to your father, the devil ... for he is a liar and the father of lies" (John 8 v 44).

Long ago, in a beautiful garden in the Middle East, Satan established himself as the archetypal false teacher and spiritual abuser. Appearing in the form of a serpent, he lured Adam and Eve to the tree of the knowledge of good and evil, the fruit of which God had commanded them not to eat. God wanted them to trust him. To obey one simple rule. But though the test was simple, the temptation proved strong.

"Did God really say, 'You must not eat from any tree in the garden'?" Satan asked, feigning astonishment.

"We may eat fruit from the trees in the garden," Eve clarified, "but God did say, 'You must not eat from the tree that is in the middle of the garden, and you must not touch it, or you will die.'"

"You will not certainly die," Satan said—and I imagine him sighing and rolling his eyes:

God knows that when you eat from it your eyes will
be opened, and you will be like God, knowing good
and evil. (Genesis 3 v 1-5)

Satan's game was very simple. He accused God, their Creator and Friend, of being a deceiver. He wanted them to distrust God and question his motives. Satan knew that if Adam and Eve felt insecure and alienated from God, they'd be vulnerable. Adam and Eve fell into sin that day, and all their descendants fell too, because they distrusted God and believed the devil. But God promised Eve he'd send her a Son to defeat Satan and restore paradise. That Son is Jesus.

The Bible sometimes refers to Satan as an accuser (Revelation 12 v 10; see also Zechariah 3 v 1). Satan told Adam and Eve that God was a liar. Like an abuser, Satan manipulates, blame-shifts, criticizes, and deceives. He wants to drown us in insecurity, anger, and guilt until we feel isolated from God's grace. He wants us to feel alone, cut off from love, doomed to failure. For someone with a loud and insistent Stranger, Satan corroborates and amplifies every accusatory, diminishing, and self-loathing fear.

But deceptions from Satan are no sign we are unloved by God. Jesus himself endured Satan's taunts. Unlike Adam, Jesus wasn't tempted in an idyllic garden brimming with fruit and flowers, in the company of his beloved wife. He was wandering in the wilderness, isolated in a desert, deprived of food, shelter, and companionship. Adam sinned in paradise, but Jesus was victorious in the wasteland. Studying the temptation of Jesus and his responses to Satan's mind games has strengthened and encouraged me during my recovery.

TAUNT ONE: DISTRUST GOD AND DO IT YOURSELF

After fasting forty days and forty nights, [Jesus] was hungry. The tempter came to him and said, "If you are the Son of God, tell these stones to become bread." Jesus answered, "It is written: 'Man shall not live on bread alone, but on every word that comes from the mouth of God.'" (Matthew 4 v 2-4)

Imagine how this experience must have felt for Jesus. Though fully God, Jesus was as human as you or me. He felt hunger, pain, and weakness. Imagine feeling like you should be dead, but not dying. After forty days of seclusion, sleeping in the wilderness, exposure to the elements, and physical deprivation, Satan comes to kick Jesus while he's down. And what does Satan say? *If you're really the Son of God, provide for yourself. If your Father won't give you food, give food to yourself. If you're really something special, let's see what you've got.*

Sound familiar? Satan told Adam to eat forbidden food. Now he's telling Jesus to eat food God didn't provide. Satan told Adam to distrust God's motives. Now he tells Jesus to distrust God's provision.

Too often my Stranger has told me to distrust God and others. He's sown insecurity, challenged whether I'm really loved, and made me doubt my value. He points out my painful experiences, asking, "Does God really care?" He shames me for feeling neglected and deprived, and pressures me to "suck it up," and suffer in silence alone.

And so we think to ourselves, "God has abandoned me. I'm on my own, isolated. I've got to take care of myself, even if that means breaking some rules." The Stranger doesn't know how to trust, and he doesn't understand mercy or contentment. He sets impossible standards and creates hoops for us to jump through. He says, "God helps those who help themselves," and "If God loves you, he wants you to be happy, so this little sin won't be a big deal."

How did Jesus respond to this mind game? He quoted Deuteronomy 8, where Moses told the Israelites:

> *Remember how the LORD your God led you all the way in the wilderness these forty years, to humble and test you in order to know what was in your heart, whether or not you would keep his commands. He humbled you, causing you to hunger and then feeding you with manna, which neither you nor your ancestors had known, to teach you that man does not live on bread alone but on every word that comes from the mouth of the LORD. (Deuteronomy 8 v 2-3)*

Jesus knows that his current suffering, feelings of isolation, and physical deprivation are no sign that God has abandoned him. He knows there's a bigger plan and a greater goal than his instant gratification in that moment. He refuses to bend the rules and doesn't fall for Satan's tricks. Unlike Adam, Jesus calls out Satan's lies and throws his manipulation in his face.

Jesus is effectively saying to him, *Earthly trials and discomforts don't disprove God's love or involvement. You advise me to find relief from my suffering in ways other than what God permits, but I will trust him, for his truth and goodness are ample to sustain me. I'm his Son whether I'm hungry or full, alone or with friends, rich or poor. I'm defined by the love of God, not by my circumstances or your opinion.*

TAUNT TWO: IF GOD REALLY LOVED YOU...

> *Then the devil took him to the holy city and had him stand on the highest point of the temple. "If you are*

*the Son of God," he said, "throw yourself down. For
it is written: 'He will command his angels concerning
you, and they will lift you up in their hands, so that
you will not strike your foot against a stone.'" Jesus
answered him, "It is also written: 'Do not put the
Lord your God to the test.'" (Matthew 4 v 5-7)*

Like the Stranger inside, Satan doesn't give up easily. He te-
naciously continues to challenge Jesus, adapting his tactics
just enough to be confusing. It's not that Satan doesn't know
who Jesus is. It's not that he has any genuine desire to see
Jesus perform a miracle. Satan is the quintessential gaslighting abuser. He gets a kick out of tormenting the human side
of Jesus, which is capable of feeling exhaustion, despair, and
pain. Satan's second temptation demonstrates just how manipulative and cruel he really is. He knows Jesus is starving.
He knows Jesus is lonely and run down, so he lashes out
with the bitterest words imaginable.

Throw yourself off a roof, he says. *Kill yourself. If God really
loves you, and has bigger plans for you, you'll be fine. God will
save you, and then I'll stop tormenting you. So, do it. Jump!*

This lie is often rehashed by the Stranger Inside. *If God
really loves you, why are you suffering? Surely, if he truly cared,
he wouldn't let anything bad happen to you. He wouldn't have
let you marry a violent man. He wouldn't have let you be born
to a narcissistic mother. He wouldn't have let your uncle do that
to you. He wouldn't let you become suicidal. If God loved you,
and you loved God, these bad things wouldn't happen.*

Like Satan, the Stranger loves setting up tests for God to
pass, but Jesus shows us the perfect response. It's not our
place to ask God to prove his goodness, faithfulness, or ex-
istence. He already did when he gave us his word. In the
Bible, God chronicles his quest to redeem his people, from
the fall of mankind to the victory of Christ. He calls us to

walk by faith, not wallow in disbelief, seeking for signs. And when we feel our faith is weak or even nonexistent, we can call on God's Spirit to give us faith.

Again, Jesus defies Satan's mockery. There's no need for the Son of God to take a literal leap of faith. He essentially retorts, *I know who I am, and I know my Father. You know who I am. I am God. Don't test my patience.*

Just so, we can rebuff the Stranger Inside, saying, "I know who God is. He is loving and faithful. My circumstances are no indication that he is not with me."

TAUNT THREE: EVIL IS IN CHARGE

Again, the devil took him to a very high mountain and showed him all the kingdoms of the world and their splendor. "All this I will give you," he said, "if you will bow down and worship me." Jesus said to him, "Away from me, Satan! For it is written: 'Worship the Lord your God, and serve him only.'"
(Matthew 4 v 8-10)

Here's where Satan shows us all his cards. He falsely claims, *I own this world. I rule these nations. I'm in control and I'll give you what you want if you please me and praise me. You don't need to go through all that your Father has laid out for you—suffering, rejection, death. Walk my way and you can have all that you want, with none of the cost, none of the struggle.*

Satan offers Jesus a shortcut around the cross with a price-tag of sin. Satan knows the Creator owns all creation. He himself is a parasite that God could wipe off the face of the earth any second. In his insolence, Satan tells a holy God to pretend evil is in charge.

My Stranger inside echoes a similar lie. *I'm the voice of experience you can't get rid of. Your best bet is to let me guide you, because I own you, and if you tell anyone about me, they'll think you're crazy. Give up on your relationships with God and other people. Trusting me is easier and safer than trusting them.*

But the Stranger doesn't own us any more than Satan owns Jesus or the world. God owns us. We are responsible for our words and actions, and our abusers are responsible for theirs. Unlike Christ, we lack the divine ability to always see through mind games and manipulation, especially when it's coming from within as the effects of abuse echo from our past. Our finite nature leaves us vulnerable to things like fear, worry, and depression. That's why the Stranger inside is often so dangerous and so difficult to resist.

Nevertheless, we can take a page out of Jesus' book and respond to the Stranger, "Be quiet! Leave me alone! I am loved by God and will do what is right, no matter how much you mock or degrade me."

Just as Satan tempted Adam, plunging humanity into sin, so he hoped to tempt Jesus, throwing wrenches into God's redemptive plan. Perhaps if Satan had known that Jesus came to die, he wouldn't have been so eager to get him crucified. But in the wilderness, after Satan's third and final taunt, Jesus told him, "Away from me!" and the accuser swiftly departed.

A BETTER VOICE THAT WILL NOT LEAVE US

In order to silence the Stranger inside, we must first recognize it for what it is: echoes of an abuser who can no longer harm us—aftershocks from a trauma that shook our past. But then it needs to be replaced by something good—something true and something empowering. When lies threaten to drown us in poison, the gospel of Jesus Christ is oxygen, anti-venom, and a life-jacket to our souls. It's what enables us to contradict the lies. It's how we can see past the lens that is coloring our life and relationships in shades of pain, and fling that lens away.

So, tell God what the Stranger is telling you. Confide your most intimate fears, insecurities, weaknesses, and temptations through prayer: your nightmares, flashbacks, doubts, and paranoias. Don't hold back. He's God. He can take it. You can be honest with him.

Ask God to take away your pain and shame. He is the therapist who doesn't take notes, the doctor who prescribes his own healing Spirit. He is the friend who understands completely and never judges those who love him. Our Great Physician, Wonderful Counselor, and Mighty Comforter shows up when we're weak, but, unlike the Stranger, he offers peace.

Jesus came to destroy the works of the devil, rendering Satan's accusations against God's people impotent. I love this promise, which he made the night before he died:

> *And I will ask the Father, and he will give you*
> *another advocate to help you and be with you*
> *forever—the Spirit of truth. The world cannot accept*
> *him, because it neither sees him nor knows him. But*
> *you know him, for he lives with you and will be in*
> *you. I will not leave you as orphans; I will come to*
> *you. (John 14 v 16-18)*

Just as Jesus responded to Satan, we can respond to the Stranger inside, silencing the voice harassing us. For about a year I made a habit of contradicting the voice, both silently in my head, and aloud when I was alone.

If the Stranger said, "Your husband only stays with you because he'd feel guilty leaving," I'd respond, "That's a lie. Jason loves me and has given me no reason to doubt his sincerity."

If the Stranger said, "You'll never succeed at anything; resign yourself to a life of failure, because that's what you are, a failure," I'd respond, "I was created by God, so to insult me is to insult his work. I don't write, sing, or play piano in order to justify my value as a human being, but because God designed me to glorify him and take joy in these things. Even my weaknesses are used to demonstrate his love and mercy."

If the Stranger said, "If you don't forgive your abuser, Jesus won't forgive you; that means tolerating their sin, letting them near your kids, and pretending you're happy and safe when you're not," I'd respond, "I'm not angry. God has graciously healed me of that pain and freed me of that burden. But God wants me to protect my children, and if anyone hinders my relationship with God, or my ability to be a godly wife and mother, I can, like Jesus, tell my abuser to go away."

The idea of talking back to the Stranger inside may sound odd. Technically, you're just talking to yourself, as everyone does from time to time. The Stranger is your pain: it's your mind giving voice to insecurities, fears, and anxieties, echoing the hurtful words of false accusers. Traumatized or not, depressed or happy, anxious or confident, we all have inner conflicts and internal dialogs. But for those of us whose Stranger parrots our abuser, talking back can seem terrifying. However, once you start standing up for yourself to yourself, you'll feel empowered.

If you place your faith in Christ, you can proactively flaunt God's grace. Brag about your identity in Jesus because of his redemptive work on your behalf. Even when the Stranger is silent, take initiative to bolster yourself in prayer. Rehearse the gospel to yourself. Sometimes I write it on my bathroom mirror in dry-erase marker, so it's the first thing I see in the morning and the last thing I see before bed. I know of a woman who preaches the gospel to herself every morning in the shower. That's a great way to start the day!

Acknowledge your achievements, and thank God for the strengths and attributes he gave you.

Invest time in maintaining your physical, emotional, and spiritual health. Get into the habit of showing yourself mercy as God has shown you mercy. Allow yourself joy and dignity, because you are valuable as an image-bearer of him. Don't measure your value by where you have been but by where you are going. Claim Jesus as your Savior, make him your boast, and rest in the assurance that he is Lord over heaven and earth. Satan himself is subject to him. You can say to your Stranger what Job said to his judgmental, accusatory friends:

> *How long will you torment me*
> *and crush me with words?*
> *Ten times now you have reproached me;*
> *shamelessly you attack me …*
> *I know that my redeemer lives,*
> *and that in the end he will stand on the*
> *earth. (Job 19 v 2-3, 25)*

PRAYER

Lord, silence the Stranger inside. Help me see through the lies of depression and fears of anxiety. Give me peace resting in you, knowing that you made me and you don't make mistakes. Fill me with confidence and assurance of your love. Replace my cynical inner voice with your promises as told in your word. I know my Great Physician lives. You are my cure from sin and pain.

> *Then the devil left him, and angels came and*
> *attended him. (Matthew 4 v 11)*

10. OUT OF THE VALLEY OF THE SHADOW OF DEATH

Dark thoughts, like ships, sailed across her
*   mind:*
"What will mother do when she finds me?"
And in her hand the key to freedom,
"But what will freedom leave behind me?"
*   (The Bedroom Door)*

As I wandered through the wilderness of my world, I became acquainted with two demons. The name of the first was Depression, and the name of her lover was Suicide. These ancient spirits have plagued mankind for thousands of years, and while they may employ different tactics when stalking different prey, their end game is always the same. Although known to millions, they have within them a strange power. For, when they are with you, they are visible to you alone.

Upon my first meeting Depression, she seemed kind. She pitied me. She sympathized. As we walked, she told me about how much greater my pain was than that of anyone else she'd ever known. She told me she'd help me get through the confusion. She wasn't an overly beautiful woman—just pretty enough to be pleasant and homely enough to put one at ease. Her eyes were understanding, her voice comforting, and her fragrance addicting. She'd be there for me. She'd warn me anytime someone tried to trick me into believing they cared. She'd protect me. She was Wisdom. She was Experience. She was Love.

"Where are you going?" Depression asked curiously as she joined me along the way.

"I am going to make a better life for myself," I replied. "I'm going to try to find Happiness."

She smiled understandingly, lazily twirling her hair. With a wink and a nod, Suicide fell in behind us. She glanced at him, rolled her eyes, and gave me a look as if to insinuate what a mischievous flirt she thought he was. I laughed, and he smiled.

"You've worked so hard already," she said, returning to our conversation. "You must be so tired. What you really need is a break. You need to rest and not worry about things for a while. Surely, you don't plan to struggle upstream forever."

"I am very tired," I conceded, "but I have to keep trying. I cannot give up."

"Why does nobody else help you?" she asked curiously. "Your friends and family seem so caught up in their own lives."

"They have their own troubles," I reasoned. "Also, I don't do a very good job of asking for help when I need it."

"True," said she, though she sounded doubtful. "Perhaps they haven't noticed how withdrawn you are because they're too wrapped up in themselves. That would be understandable, I suppose. We must forgive them. Of course, they may also find your withdrawal to be a relief. After all, your sorrow runs deep. Some people, unless they really love you a lot, are hesitant to get into the mess of someone else's damage.

"Still, it's not too much to ask for a little appreciation and respect, is it?" Depression chattered on. "It seems to me you get taken for granted more often than not. If they truly appreciated you, you'd think they'd notice how much you've been struggling and be more open to associating with you, even though they know you are in pain."

"I'm under-appreciated because I rarely bring anything that's not tainted by pain to the table," I retorted.

Depression's voice was pleasantly happy and vindicating, but her words were filling me with a vague anxiety. Now she watched me silently, apparently waiting, so I continued.

"I get taken for granted a lot because I'm eager to please," I said. "People have come to expect me to be accommodating. I don't want to burden my friends with my pain. I avoid telling anyone when I'm sad because I feel sad so frequently. My baggage isn't anything new, and I don't want to become that person who is known for being a constant drag. It's really my fault I'm misunderstood. I'm difficult to be around, and I don't communicate well. My friends don't mean to overlook me. It's just the way things are."

"I'm sure you're right," she said, nodding. "I don't know, I just see your friends with their happy marriages, their loving parents, and their positive thinking. It's such a beautiful and joyous thing. Their kids are lucky to have grandparents who are plugged in. It would be nice if your kids did."

"They could have," I agreed bitterly. "Sometimes people love their problems more than they love their own families. They make you choose between them and the health of your marriage or your children's wellbeing. I did what I had to."

"Oh, for certain," she agreed. Then suddenly she laughed merrily. "Did you see Susan's mother at church again? She seems to be staying for a very long visit. It must be wonderful to have her helping around the house and spending time with the children."

"Yes," said I, growing darker. "I'm sure it's very nice."

"But really," she continued, seemingly unaware of my declining mood, "it's not your parents' fault they're so messed up. Their parents before them were complete wrecks."

"That's no excuse," I said defensively. "If anything, a person who knows what it's like to grow up in an abusive home should be extra careful not to be abusive themselves. They know how it feels. I could have handled broken parents. I could have understood parents who were struggling. I cannot understand a parent who intentionally and persistently hurt me. I cannot understand a parent unwilling to take any risks to help me or protect me."

"You're right," she said, becoming grave. "You're absolutely right. I'm sorry I was so flippant. They knew exactly what they were doing. The silver lining is, even though you're broken and in pain, you can try to be a decent mother to your children. They won't be abused at least."

"If my childhood had been healthier," I said, "if I hadn't felt so trapped, preyed upon, and frightened for the first 20 years of my life, I could have been so much more than merely decent."

"Yes, you could have been a happier, stronger, and less broken mother," she agreed wistfully. "You could've been the sort of person who inspires and motivates: the kind other people want to be like. However, perhaps your pain will help prepare your children to cope with their own lives. They'll see your brokenness and know it's OK to cry, OK to fail, and it's OK to be broken. There's a real freedom in that."

"I don't want them to see that," I whispered.

"It can't be helped, my dear," she said consolingly, putting her arm around my shoulders. "This is who we are. Our pain is our heritage. We leave our children what we can. Some leave money and houses, but money and houses are just material things. You're leaving them an emotional legacy. Someday, if one of your daughters marries a wife-beater, she'll know exactly how to live with him, and it will be all because of you."

That's when her lover, Suicide, finally spoke up. He'd been walking with us all along, watching, like a shadow that sees all. He had a beautiful face and a beautiful voice. It was deep and sensual. He too understood me perfectly. There was no shame with him. There was no fear. There was only mercy. There was only freedom. He told me he'd never let me be vulnerable again. He'd guard my heart from caring too much about people who were just going to let me down. He promised he'd make sure my loved ones felt peace. They'd be comforted knowing I was at peace, and I was finally free.

"Sometimes," he said, "the most loving thing we can do for someone is step out of their lives."

I felt slightly nauseous at these words.

"That's exactly what I told my father," I said, "when I told him his lies were damaging me too much."

"Yes," Suicide replied. "You are very wise and very strong. You do what is right, even when it hurts. It is one of your finest qualities."

I thought about this for a moment.

"Do you think my kids would be better off without me in their lives?" I asked.

Suicide seemed to give this some thought. He looked at me, as if to sum me up, and then glanced thoughtfully back down at the road before his feet. It was as if he was weighing his words very carefully, as if he didn't want to hurt me.

"You're a kind person," he said with the solemn air of a physician about to deliver a terminal diagnosis. "Because of that, I feel morally obligated to be completely transparent with you. It's not your fault, but you have a contagious kind of damage. It affects everything you touch, everything you say, and everything you do. It changes your kids' lives in ways we cannot even begin to predict. And, since we're being so open and honest with each other, don't you think your husband would be happier with a wife who is less broken?"

I thought about this for some time. Suicide and Depression patiently waited as I turned things over in my head. About this time, we came to a rocky area shaded by trees, and since I'd grown weary and troubled, we sat down to rest.

"Yes," I finally answered, picking up a fallen leaf and twirling it idly between my fingers. I smiled through my pain. "He's young and handsome. He'll be able to find a new wife fairly easily I think. I'm not sure what he'll do with the children in the interim though. He works full-time."

"You have so many friends," Depression interjected, slipping back into her merry tone. "They'd easily take turns babysitting, and pretty soon the children will be starting school and attending summer camps. It won't be too much of an inconvenience. I'm sure he'll understand, my dear. In the end, he'll know you did it for him. It's what's best for his happiness."

A tear slipped down my cheek, though I didn't sob or make any other signs of crying.

"In the long run," continued Suicide, pretending not to notice my sadness, "they'd have a happy mother: someone who laughs a lot, has the emotional energy to take them to the park and to play-dates any day of the week, who doesn't have down-days and up-days, and can be depended upon to be balanced and positive."

"But where will I go?" I asked. "What will I do? There is nothing for me in this world without my children. I don't want to date or get married again. And my husband will follow me. He'll find me."

At this, Suicide scooted closer. He put his arm around my shoulders, kissed me gently on the forehead, and looked down on me lovingly.

"He will never find you if you go where he cannot

follow," he whispered. "Your death would make him sad for a time, but after a few weeks, it would bring him such peace. He'd never have to worry about what mood you're going to be in. He'd never wonder what state the house is in or whether you've had the energy to have dinner ready when he gets home. He'd never have to question whether you're disciplining the kids out of love or out of some predisposition toward abuse. You and I both know you're a wonderful mother in your heart, but sometimes truly loving someone means letting them go."

Depression sighed and stood up, as if she was uncomfortable with all this weighty talk. She paced a few times, then stopped in front of me, and shook her head.

"It's the right thing to do," she said resignedly. "It's the loving thing to do."

"It's the strong thing to do," agreed Suicide. "You've been weak all your life, taking abuse. All your attempts to fight back have been complete failures. You've tried multiple times to fix yourself and failed, but it's not too late. It's never too late to do what's right. This damage you have isn't skin deep. It permeates to your very soul. You will never mature beyond it. You will never be loved, except by those who pity you, and are willing to suffer for you and by you. I know it's difficult, but it's time to be realistic about yourself. This damage will always be with you. Whether you die today or in fifty years, you will take it with you to your grave. It's the damage you spread between now and then that has to be our concern."

Just then, around a blind bend in the road, there came a man. As he saw us, he began to run. His skin was sunkissed and leathery, his hair was a black mass of windblown curls, and his hands were coarse and calloused as if from manual labor. He approached us, and there was compassion but also a severe earnestness in his dark eyes. As he reached us, I stood, and he clasped my hands in his.

"You do not have to die," he said, slightly out of breath. "Another has already died for you. He paid the price for all your sin. He chose you: before the foundation of the world was laid, he chose you to be his sister, the daughter of his Father—to be the wife of your husband and the mother of your children. He didn't choose a happier or less flawed woman; he chose you. Your role in this world has been ordained since before the dawn of time. You are exactly who and where you are supposed to be. The Son of God has died for you, and the Spirit of God is with you. I have seen it. It is finished. There's no need to isolate yourself from God any longer. It is finished."

I pulled my hands out of his, surprised. "But I'm a millstone holding my family down," I cried. "How can I go on tormenting them with my pain? I'm a blight."

"Do you really think," he asked incredulously, "that your family would be better off without the mother whom God designed and created specifically for them? Do you really think your story of healing and redemption following such terrible pain and near death is not worth telling? Your damage is no longer something to be ashamed of. Rather, it is evidence—it is proof—that the God of the universe is with you, and he is more powerful than death. He's a profoundly healing, loving, merciful, miracle-working Savior. Your life is not a story of pain; it's the story of his grace. You are not forsaken."

As soon as he had said this, I turned and looked. Depression and Suicide had vanished. It was as if they had never been there at all. The only evidence of our conversation was a bruise on my arm where Suicide's eager hand had gripped me. It's strange, because when he was with me he was so gentle and kind. Somehow, in my mesmerized state, I'd overlooked his crushing strength.

Still, I had doubts. "What about my own mother and

father?" I asked the stranger. "Were they designed specifically to be my parents? Because that didn't work out very well."

"God designed them, but he did not design their sin," he said. "He wept over your pain. And he brought you through it, didn't he? Nevertheless, everything in your life—your victimization, sorrow, depression, fears, and yes, even your rage—has been sweeping you like a rushing river toward this very moment. Like a flower that springs from decay and death, or a diamond formed in utter darkness, God can cause the works of evildoers to backfire, using them to bring about beauty and good. Like Jesus, who rose from a murderous death to walk out of the tomb, you too by his power can walk out of this darkness.

"The God who created order from chaos is working a new creation in you," he continued. "By his grace you have overcome the demons, Depression and Suicide. You have been victorious over the darkness that haunts us all. Jesus said, 'Take up your cross and follow me,' and you have struggled along in his footsteps, just as he struggled toward Golgotha. Rather than view your pain as the flood that drowns you, view it as the tomb he is guiding you out of. Take comfort, daughter of God, for Jesus has once again vanquished death in you."

This time I took his hand in mine. Together, we looked back upon the valley, which now lay stretched below us. And that's when I recognized it for what it was: the Valley of the Shadow of Death.

"Who are you?" I asked the man, "and where did you come from?"

"I am your understanding of all the apostles and prophets. I am Psalm 23 and the Lord's Prayer. I am King David and Isaiah and Paul. I am your memories of the word of God, and the unbidden recollection God slips into your subconscious during times of great need."

"So," I said, feeling rather confused, "you're not real?"

"I'm as real as you are," he laughed. "I'm a work of God's Spirit: the part of you that hears God. I'm sorry I've been so absent lately. I lost my way in the trees."

Several years have gone by since that metaphorical walk, and several times I have returned to the Valley. Suicide rarely comes around anymore, though sometimes I catch a glimpse of him, stalking me in the distance. Depression occasionally pays me a visit, but Suicide is not always with her. Unlike his manipulative lover, Suicide cannot wander beyond the confines of the Valley. Unfortunately, Depression is often accompanied by her husband, Anxiety. While she's not a faithful wife, and loves to flirt with Suicide, Anxiety seems far too obsessed with tormenting me to care.

So, you see, Depression and Suicide appear to be our friends. They're not fearful predators, as pop culture would have us believe, or scary monsters who make us feel hunted. They aren't the darkness we're pressed into against our will. They seem wonderful. They feel like solutions. They appear reasonable. But they lie.

What saved me from killing myself was never self-worth. In my teens and early twenties, I had no dreams of a better tomorrow or hope of feeling joy again. I survived because I didn't want to destroy other people's lives. I wanted to spare whoever found my body from the trauma. That's how I'm alive, writing this to you.

The other reason I chose life was because I realized heaven is real, and heaven is for me. These days, I realize this more than ever. When God promised his people, "I will never leave you nor forsake you," he left no room for exceptions (Hebrews 13 v 5, ESV). With David, I can say to God:

*Even though I walk through the valley of the shadow
of death,*
    I will fear no evil,
for you are with me. (Psalm 23 v 4, ESV)

Because my faith rests in Jesus—because his Spirit is planted like an anchor in my heart—no storm of life, however dark or violent, can rip me from his grasp.

From the moment of my conception, he was knitting me together (Psalm 139 v 13-16). He set my faith alight and sheltered it as one shelters a candle from the breeze. Every day of my life, every breath and good work, has been planned out and ordained from before the dawn of time (Ephesians 2 v 10). Who am I to cut my life short? Who am I to question his purpose? And the knowledge that there's an appointed time—a moment written in eternity when I shall meet my Father face to face—makes my waiting time in this mortal realm feel temporary and bearable, and the anticipation brings joy.

Sometimes we get so used to disappointment, sorrow, and death that it's difficult to believe the exact opposite is what awaits us. We expect tragedy and pain, making joy and peace seem like a fairy tale. But Jesus—who we know is real—came down from heaven to be born a human. We know Jesus is God, and Jesus would not lie to us or give us false hope. God's Son lived in heaven before he lay in a manger, and he reigns in heaven again now.

Whenever we start to feel that our lives are futile and doomed—when we cannot believe heaven is real or meant for us—we can cling to what Jesus knows firsthand. For he said:

*My Father's house has many rooms; if that were not
so, would I have told you that I am going there to
prepare a place for you? (John 14 v 2)*

You can take comfort knowing that Jesus is God, Jesus does not lie, and if heaven were a fairy tale, he would not have called it the home of his children. This world may be a dark tunnel at times, but the Light of the world, Jesus Christ, is at the end. Whether he returns within my lifetime or I die before he comes, I will see him face to face in not too long a time. Our suffering here is put in perspective when we fix our eyes on him.

PRAYER

As the deer pants for flowing streams, so pants my soul for you, oh God. My soul thirsts for the living God. When will I come to see you face to face? My tears have fed me day and night, while enemies mock and shame. In the darkest night of my soul, I remember you. Deep calls unto deep at the roar of your waterfalls; the waves of your oceans rush over me. Command your steadfast love to overwhelm me, and even at the bottom of the sea, your hope will be with me. Like a deadly cancer in my bones, my agony taunts me even in my sleep. Do not let my soul be cast down. Calm me, heal me, comfort me, reassure me. Bless me with hope in you, so I may praise you as my salvation.

(Based on Psalm 42)

11. RECOVERING FATHERHOOD

How like glass my heart is shattered
Broken pieces on the floor,
Memories of love are tainted
Despair opens wide his door,
Calling me, "Child, I'll embrace you
Like your father never could,
I will hold you fast forever
Like your father never would."

Israel's first king, Saul, was pleasing to the eye. In fact, there was not a man in all Israel more tall and handsome than he (1 Samuel 9 v 2). The people loved Saul's outward appearance, and his royal status made them feel powerful and trendy.

Then along came Goliath, nearly ten feet tall, to tower over Saul. The Philistine warrior terrified the king, who offered his daughter and prize money to anyone who could kill Israel's enemy. When a plucky young shepherd boy offered to fight, Saul scoffed at his small stature and youth, but David's trust wasn't in appearances. He killed Goliath, and all of Israel praised his valor.

When Saul realized God's favor was with David and heard the people celebrating David's victories more than his, he grew jealous (1 Samuel 18 v 6-8). He began to see David as a threat. He gave David his daughter in marriage, hoping to manipulate the younger man (v 17, 20-21). He even tried to convince his own son—David's best friend, Jonathan—to help murder him (19 v 1; 20 v 31).

But, like many children of abusive fathers, Jonathan played the human shield. He served as a buffer between his loved ones and his violent parent. Despite struggling with denial that his dad was capable of murder, Jonathan warned David and helped him flee the king's wrath.

And so, Saul became a biblical example of the spiritually corrosive nature of abusers. He fed his selfishness and anger until they consumed him, twisting his mind and destroying his family:

> *Saul's anger flared up at Jonathan and he said to him, "You son of a perverse and rebellious woman! Don't I know that you have sided with the son of Jesse to your own shame and to the shame of the mother who bore you? As long as the son of Jesse lives on this earth, neither you nor your kingdom will be established. Now send someone to bring him to me, for he must die!"*
>
> *"Why should he be put to death? What has he done?" Jonathan asked his father. But Saul hurled his spear at him to kill him. Then Jonathan knew that his father intended to kill David. (1 Samuel 20 v 30-33)*

Jonathan witnessed his dad's deteriorating mental state. Saul degraded Jonathan to his face, confided paranoia, and tried to draw him into his wicked plans. But it wasn't until Saul tried to murder his own son that Jonathan's denial fell away. Only then did Jonathan know that his father really intended to kill David.

How must Jonathan have felt as he helped his dearest friend flee his own murderous father? How must he have wrestled inwardly, deciding whether to stay in his father's house or escape alongside David? Yet even after witnessing Saul's violence, hearing his threats, and confronting his evil, Jonathan didn't leave. He remained devoted to his father and was eventually slain in battle at his father's side.

I've often wondered how Jonathan felt as he lay dying in that field, surrounded by his fallen brothers.

What was his understanding of fatherhood? Was he comforted by knowing the peace he'd soon experience once he reached his real Father's house? Did he struggle to imagine God as a loving Father? Could he see past Saul's sins to understand what fatherhood was intended to be? Or did he fear that the God he was about to meet would be unpredictably angry or unaccountably disappointed, or that he'd apathetically abandon him?

REFLECTIONS IN THE DARK

I find it easy to understand Jonathan's desperate desire to believe his dad would turn out OK. Even after reality hit, he didn't leave his abusive father. Modern victims are no different. "Surely," we think, "we can patch things up." It's amazing how self-deceptive our hearts can be when lies are preferable to truth. But then something horrible happens. With a jolt we realize our dad isn't getting better. These sins aren't one-time events or mistakes.

Oftentimes, children with abusive fathers blame their mothers for their dad's sin. "Why didn't she help him overcome his darkness? Why didn't she protect me from it?" Heartbroken sons sometimes instinctively see their mothers in other women, sabotaging their relationships with them because they don't believe they can trust women to protect or support them. Heartbroken daughters sometimes react against all men, seeing their dad's predilections everywhere and losing their ability to trust.

But we cannot let sinful people inform our perception of a holy God. We cannot let dysfunctional relationships inform how we view our relationship with our Creator. Our triune God—Father, Son, and Spirit—is a relational God. In the Bible, he describes himself and his people in relational terms.

God considers believers to be his family (Matthew 12 v 48-50). He calls himself the Father of his children (1 John 3 v 1). In his care for his people, God says he is like a loving mother comforting her babies (Isaiah 66 v 13). The Father calls Jesus his Son (Luke 3 v 22), and the Son calls himself our Brother (Mark 3 v 34) and Friend (Luke 5 v 20). Jesus is also pictured as a Bridegroom (Isaiah 62 v 5), and the church—all those who love him as their Lord and Savior—is his beloved Bride (Ephesians 5 v 25-27). He's the Husband of his people (Revelation 19 v 7-8).

For better or for worse, we all have preconceived notions of what these relationships mean, based on our experiences. For those with healthy families and marriages, we're pointed toward the greater reality we can enjoy with God. For those who've suffered abuse from a parent, spouse, sibling, or other loved one, the very words God uses to describe himself may be weighted down with baggage and pain. You've probably heard of the antichrist—the false teacher and fake savior mentioned in the Bible who distorts the gospel and leads people astray. In order to detach my experiences with my dad from my perception of God, I had to think of my abusive father as an antifather. Like Saul, he's a father who embodies everything my Father God is not: a conman posing as a paternal figure, a tyrant playing king, God's nasty little doppelganger.

We must not allow an abusive father to define our concept of fatherhood. We must not allow an abusive spouse to define our understanding of marital love. An abusive pastor or priest does not represent what God means when he calls himself our Shepherd. An abuser's dysfunction cannot inform our perception of God's perfection. Otherwise, it's like trusting a mudpuddle to adequately reflect a rainbow, or a tarnished spoon to mirror the beauty of the starry sky. The reflection is distorted; clouded beyond recognition.

I've had to redefine my ideas of husband, father, and even masculinity. I've had to recover my sense of wonder at the fatherhood of God. It's imperative that he, and no one else, defines what he means when he calls himself, "Father."

GOD-DEFINED FATHERHOOD

There are no words to fully describe the depth, profundity, or passion of Father God's devotion to his children. Trying to explain it is like trying to describe the vastness of outer space or the hotness of the sun, or how long eternity is. I can catch a small glimpse of his love when I ponder his investment in me, his patience with me, his faithfulness to me, and his forgiveness of me.

1. God's Investment

My Father in heaven invests himself wholeheartedly in me. God has personally poured his blood, sweat, and Spirit into me.

His time: God spent thousands of years, working through hundreds of people, to write the Bible, God's love letter to me. God isn't merely a witness to history; he is the composer, orchestrator, and conductor—he is an active participant in it. He's invested in my life. I may not always feel him, but just because we can't sense something doesn't mean that it isn't real.

His blood: In the fullness of time, God sent his Son into the world to become human—just like you and me, yet still fully God—to live a perfectly sinless, miraculous life. He took my place, trading his own life as the ransom for a soul held hostage by Satan. The sacrifice of Jesus wasn't an impersonal email blast or shot in the dark. He died specifically with me in mind. He bought me with "his own blood" (Acts 20 v 28). He rose from the dead, and so I can rise too. Even amid the bliss of heaven, Jesus thinks of me and prays for me by name (Romans 8 v 34).

His Spirit: After the Father glorified Jesus in heaven, he poured out his Spirit upon his Son's siblings. The Spirit works in the hearts of all God's children, growing us in wisdom, maturity, goodness, and healing. He is the Giver of faith and hope. He is the whisper of perseverance and desire to overcome. He is Recovery.

The Father didn't secure my forgiveness but then say, "You're on your own, kid. Good luck!" No. He came to dwell in me. He's always working, always healing, always acting. Like a master engineer, he tinkers, cleans, and oils the cogs of my heart to build me to be stronger and more reflective of him. He is personally, constantly, and passionately involved in the inner workings of me. There's nothing he doesn't care about—nothing I cannot speak to him about.

2. God's Faithfulness

Consider Jonah. Jonah had the benefit of being a prophet. He audibly heard God speak to him. Nevertheless, Jonah blatantly refused to do what God told him. He would not go to Nineveh and tell a people he hated about the forgiveness of God. Instead, Jonah fled from God (Jonah 1 v 1-3).

Did God give up on Jonah? Did he resort to a different prophet? No. He worked with Jonah, albeit much to Jonah's dismay, and in an incredibly comical way. First, God sent a storm to rock the boat Jonah was fleeing on. It must have been a strange storm because it terrified the sailors yet did not wake Jonah from sleep. The sailors rushed below deck, roused Jonah from his nap, and, upon learning that he was fleeing from God, chucked him into the churning sea (v 4-15).

Did God abandon Jonah then? Did he say, "You got yourself into this one, Jonah!" No. Instead of letting Jonah drown, God did the absolute last thing most people would ever think of.

He didn't send a second boat. He didn't send a life preserver or a wave to wash him ashore. He sent a freakishly large fish (v 17). It was as if God was saying, *Jonah, you're behaving ridiculously. Now something extraordinarily ridiculous is going to happen to you.*

Now, God doesn't send trials to crush us, and he doesn't view our failings as reasons to disown us. Rather, he walks through trials with us the way a shepherd guides a lamb through wolf-infested wilds. Bad things happen to loving and faithful people all the time. Look at Jonathan. Look at Jesus. Unlike us, Jonah had the rare honor of conversing with God, yet he fled from God and rejected his job as prophet. Despite this, God didn't lose his temper. He didn't strike Jonah dead or replace him with a better servant. He didn't let Jonah drown or give up on him. God was faithful even when Jonah was not.

Thanks to the story of Jonah, and many others like him, we know God is ready, willing, and able to forgive all our wrongdoings. We may veer off course. We may flee from God, fall into temptation, and be swallowed alive by sin. Yet our faults are no match for his love. Our failings are no obstacle to his immense grace; our damage is no hindrance to his Spirit:

In all that has happened to us, you have remained righteous; you have acted faithfully, while we acted wickedly. (Nehemiah 9 v 33)

3. God's Patience
Outside God's faithfulness, the most difficult concept for me to grasp is God's patience. I'm used to a father who acts irritated no matter how hard I try, and disinterested or cynical no matter what I achieve. Believing that God will forgive my sin and see Jesus' righteousness instead of my sin is a thing too amazing to imagine. But it's true.

Remember Jesus' story about a wandering sheep in Luke 15. Leaving the safety of the flock, the sheep strays into the territory of wolves: open country, treacherous hills, rocky Middle-Eastern wasteland. But the shepherd leaves his flock safely grazing in the pasture and searches for his lost sheep. When he finds it, he doesn't scream and curse and jump up and down. He doesn't lash out and beat the sheep or abandon it to the wolves. Instead he rejoices, lifts his lost lamb high upon his shoulders, and joyfully carries it home.

Just so, Jesus says, there will be more rejoicing in heaven over one sinner who repents than over many righteous people who never wander at all. Though we wander, our God seeks and finds us. He is a mighty Warrior who saves. He greatly delights in his children and will no longer rebuke us. He will calm us with his love and rejoice over us with singing (Zephaniah 3 v 17).

4. God's Forgiveness

> The LORD is compassionate and gracious,
>   slow to anger, abounding in love …
> For as high as the heavens are above the earth,
>   so great is his love for those who fear [live in awe
>   of] him;
> as far as the east is from the west,
>   so far has he removed our transgressions from us.
> As a father has compassion on his children,

so the LORD has compassion on those who fear him. (Psalm 103 v 8, 11-13)

God uses all things—even our weaknesses—together for our good, to mature, heal, grow, and strengthen us. God's forgiveness is so thorough that he treats us as if we had never sinned at all.

Repeatedly throughout the Bible, God tells us, "I ... am he who blots out your transgressions, for my own sake, and remembers your sins no more" (Isaiah 43 v 25). Again, in 1 John 1 v 9 we're told, "If we confess our sins, he is faithful and just and will forgive us our sins and purify us from all unrighteousness."

If you find it hard to believe that God will forgive your sins, pray and ask God to enable you to believe. Remember, he is patient, faithful, and forgiving. That's the kind of Father he is.

He's big and loving enough to handle your toughest questions, struggles, and pain. And to paraphrase C.S. Lewis, you would not be calling to him if he was not already calling to you.

WRESTLING WITH GOD

Jacob was the grandson of Abraham and the father of Joseph. Like many of us, his life was characterized by dysfunctional relationships and family drama. He was by no means a perfect man, and some of his hardships were his own fault. As he traveled through the wilderness on his way to meet his estranged brother, Esau, Jacob was attacked by a stranger. After wrestling in the darkness and the dust for hours, Jacob realized this was no mere man but God himself taking human form. By daybreak, Jacob was exhausted, and God moved to leave. But Jacob clung to him saying, "I will not let you go unless you bless me" (Genesis 32 v 26). So

God blessed Jacob and changed his name to Israel, which means, "He who wrestles, or struggles, with God."

It's a strange story, but one I find deep and relatable. Sometimes we too feel attacked by God, don't we? He makes a lot of choices we aren't happy with. He doesn't always give us the family we wanted, the job we hoped for, or the strong body we desire. He is sovereign. Even the wind and the waves obey him (Psalm 89 v 9). Yet he allowed us to walk through the Valley of the Shadow of Death. He offers forgiveness to everyone, even our abusers. How can he offer mercy to such unmerciful people?

In these times of turmoil and anxiety, we too wrestle with God. We grapple in the darkness and dust of our pain. But God doesn't wrestle with his children to defeat them. He wrestles with us to make us feel heard and realize that our frustrations have been acknowledged, to pull us back into his arms and show us he loves us, and to stop us from wandering down desolate paths or harming ourselves. After wrestling with God, Jacob ached and had a limp, but he also had God's blessing (Genesis 32 v 29, 31).

We can tell God how we feel. We can tell him that we're angry at him for seemingly abandoning us; that we don't understand why our lives are so deprived and painful; that we feel betrayed, oppressed, and neglected.

Like Job, we can moan:

> *I loathe my very life;*
> *therefore I will give free rein to my complaint*
> *and speak out in the bitterness of my soul ...*
> *Does it please you to oppress me,*
> *to spurn the work of your hands,*
> *while you smile on the plans of the wicked?*
> *(Job 10 v 1, 3)*

You can pour out your pain and rage to God. He created every molecule of every cell of your being. He strung them all together to invent you—specifically you. He knows you inside and out, so he already knows you're angry. He's patiently waiting for you to scream at him and wrestle with him so he can catch you up in his arms like an adoring father, wipe away your tears, and bless you with his love.

During my teens, I wrestled with God. In my early marriage, I wrestled harder still. I was furious at my Father for letting me be born to my father, for not protecting me from the darkness. The Bible felt like a big book of promises not intended for me, and it made me physically nauseous to read them. Prayer felt like hollow words in a pointless world where nobody listened. There were times when I dreaded church so badly I made myself throw up so I could play sick and not be pressured to go. I was ashamed of my anger at my Father, yet my anger burned like a consuming fire.

Little did I realize but I was wrestling with God. Little did I understand but, like he did for Jacob, God would bless me in the end.

GOD HATES WOLVES

Eventually, I came to the realization that God hates abuse even more than I do. Through the prophets, he repeatedly called out and condemned people who used their power, position, or strength to prey on those weaker than them. He expresses hatred of people who twist his words and use religion to meet their own ends. Jesus' fiercest warnings are reserved for hypocrites, false teachers, and those who lead God's children astray, damaging their faith:

> *If anyone causes one of these little ones—those who believe in me—to stumble, it would be better for*

them to have a large millstone hung around their
neck and to be drowned in the depths of the sea.
(Matthew 18 v 6)

"Stop bringing meaningless offerings!" God says to hypocrites in Isaiah 1:

> *I cannot bear your worthless assemblies.*
> *Your New Moon feasts and your appointed festivals*
>   *I hate with all my being.*
> *They have become a burden to me;*
>   *I am weary of bearing them.*
> *When you spread out your hands in prayer,*
>   *I hide my eyes from you;*
> *even when you offer many prayers,*
>   *I am not listening.*
> *Your hands are full of blood! (Isaiah 1 v 13b-15)*

Once I realized I was not alone in my anger over abuse—
that God himself will pour out his wrath on evildoers—
my anger lost a great deal of its bitterness. The Lord our
God is no fool. He sees through manipulators and liars
who fake godliness. He senses shallow praise and empty
prayers. Jesus warns in Matthew 7 v 15, "Watch out for
false prophets. They come to you in sheep's clothing, but
inwardly they are ferocious wolves." He wasn't speaking of
literal wolves, who tear skin and devour flesh, but spiritual
predators, who shred truth and destroy hope. "Not everyone who says to me, 'Lord, Lord,' will enter the kingdom
of heaven" (v 21).

Surely, I reasoned, the God who hates superficiality
wouldn't want me keeping secrets from him. He wouldn't
want me to lie about my anger, hiding from him out of
shame like Adam and Eve did. So, I told God I couldn't bear

reading his Bible. I told God that his promises of hope, love, and peace felt like lies to me. I told God I felt abandoned and betrayed by him. I poured out my whole broken heart.

I recalled the theology book my dad was studying before he beat me. I remembered him praying with me, reading the Bible to me, and discussing doctrine with other learned men at church. They saw nothing, but God sees all. He searches the heart and moves through our souls. He is not deceived by false teachers or abusers, nor is he defined by them.

GOD ANSWERS OUR FEARS

After years of wrestling with God—praying and pondering, seeking and praying—I finally felt like I could read the Bible again. There was no dramatic vision or tear-gushy revelation. It was a long, slow process—me and God in the darkness and dust—that led to a simple feeling of safety and a sense of acknowledgment.

It was as if I'd asked, "Where were you when I was being abused?"

And my Father replied, *I was with you all along, sustaining your faith, holding the broken pieces together, and making sure you never gave up.*

My heart said, "I'm an orphan. I have no father."

My Father answered, *Before the world was created, I chose you. Before the foundations of the universe were laid, I planned to adopt you (Ephesians 1 v 3-6).*

My heart said, "But you aren't here. I need a physical father—one who I can talk to, hug, and see."

My Father replied, *I am here. I have given you my Spirit, and so I am not living with you, but in you. I am present with you and my power is at work for you. And yes, one day, you will see me face to face (1 John 4 v 13-15; Ephesians 3 v 16).*

My heart asked, "Why did so many bad things happen to me? If you really love me, why didn't you do something?"

My Father said, *I did do something. I got you through it. I was with you at all times; I did not forsake you. I was strengthening your soul, so that you didn't give up. I was rekindling your faith, so that the spark never died. I was witnessing every evil committed against you, so someday I could give you justice (Psalm 37 v 1-9, 39-40; Philippians 1 v 6; 1 Peter 1 v 4b-7).*

My heart said, "But I have done so many stupid things. So many bad things. I've even hated you. You cannot possibly love me. I haven't been faithful to you."

My Father said, *If you were unfaithful, does that mean I'll be unfaithful too? Of course not! I am your Father. All have sinned and fallen short of my goodness. My love for you is a free gift, not a prize you can win or a trophy you must earn. I am faithful even though you are not (Psalm 136; Romans 3 v 10-26; Ephesians 2 v 1-9).*

My heart said, "But I'm so damaged. I fail again and again. All I see in myself is disappointment, imperfection, pain, and anger. How can I possibly make you happy?"

My Father said, *When I look at you, I see my Son. I see his righteousness and perfection, but I'm not blind to your pain or the wrongs done against you. Blessed are you when people revile and persecute you, and spread evil lies against you. Great is your reward in heaven, for so they persecuted me (2 Corinthians 5 v 17-18, 21; Matthew 5 v 1-12).*

My heart said, "There are so many things working against me. So many people want to tear me down."

My Father said, *No power of hell, no scheme of man, no angel or human being—nothing in the past, present, or future—can ever separate you from my love (Romans 8 v 38-39; Lamentations 3 v 22-23).*

My heart said, "I feel so much pain. Just when I think I'm getting better, something reopens my wounds, and I'm heartbroken all over again. How can I ever be whole?"

My Father reassured me: *I am the healer of the broken-hearted. I will bind up your wounds. I am the Great Physician. When a baby sparrow falls from its nest, I see it and am with it. If I never forget the short life of one fragile bird, how can I ever forget you, my beloved child? I know every bruise you've ever felt, every tear you've ever cried, every fear you've ever feared. I know every wrong ever done against you, and I love you. I love you. I will heal you and make you whole again. I will wipe away every tear from your eyes. There will be no more death, or sorrow, or suffering. All this pain will pass away—death itself will die—and I will make you new again (Psalm 34 v 15-22; 147 v 3; Luke 12 v 6-7; Revelation 21 v 1-7).*

LIKE A LOVING FATHER SHOULD

Often, we are afraid to wrestle with God. We are apprehensive about voicing the doubts we feel or of articulating the anger that we fear. Maybe we feel we need permission to express ourselves. Maybe we're afraid that putting words to our pain will make our Father angry. But our experiences with broken and warped relationships are not indicative of what God is like. Don't let an antifather—or an antimother, antispouse, antisibling, or antifriend—define your relationship with God, and prevent you enjoying him as your heavenly Father.

Your relationship with God won't be a picturesque saunter through a pristine garden. It will be an epic tale of sorrow and joy, loss and recovery, challenge and victory that will strengthen you, inspire others, and bring praise and delight to your Father. You'll rest in him and wrestle with him. You'll trust him and question him. Sometimes you'll wander off or fall into sin, only to be shepherded back by the One who is faithful when we are not. These ups and downs—your spiritual growth as you persevere by his grace, even as you wrestle with him—are what define a priceless and blessed relationship with your perfect heavenly Father.

> *My beloved, I am with you*
> *Do not fear, your God is near*
> *I will save you, I will heal you*
> *You no longer need to fear*
> *Come to me! Child, I'll embrace you*
> *Like your father never could,*
> *I will hold you fast forever*
> *Like a loving Father should.*

12. THE TRUTH ABOUT FORGIVENESS

Forgiveness is at the heart of Christianity.

However, when it comes to forgiving an abuser—particularly one who is a current threat or source or pain—things become incredibly difficult and extremely complicated. We may be emotionally unable to forgive. We may simply not want to, and that's entirely understandable. But forgiveness—when properly understood—is a peace we can hope for, a relief we can anticipate, and a joy when it arrives.

Unfortunately, it's not something we can rush. Forgiveness is a process.

When Jacob was a young man, he was jealous of his older twin brother, Esau. He wanted the birthright of the eldest heir, as well as the blessing their father would bestow on his firstborn. Rather than trust God and wait patiently for his own inheritance, Jacob used manipulation to bribe Esau out of his birthright. He conned their elderly blind father, stealing Esau's blessing (Genesis 27).

When Esau realized what Jacob had done, he was furious. He planned to murder his brother, but their mother overheard his plot and warned Jacob, so he fled. For over 20 years, the brothers did not speak, and Jacob lived in fear of Esau's retribution.

In Genesis 32, as Jacob returned to the land of his birth after all those years, messengers arrived to tell Jacob that his brother Esau and 400 men were traveling to meet him. Jacob was terrified. He anticipated an attack, violence, and his own execution. He prayed for protection from Esau, prepared gifts for him, and planned to meet him halfway in hopes of making amends and begging for forgiveness.

That night, as he camped alone, Jacob wrestled with God. When dawn arrived, he rejoined his family (32 v 22-32). Then, lifting up his eyes, Jacob saw Esau and his company approaching. He hurried ahead of his family, hoping Esau would spare their lives, and bowed himself to the ground in remorse. "But Esau ran to meet Jacob and embraced him; he threw his arms around his neck and kissed him. And they wept" (33 v 4). Through his tears Jacob begged for forgiveness, and Esau forgave Jacob.

So impressed was Jacob at Esau's love, and so humbled was he by his forgiveness, that he said, "If I have found favor in your eyes, accept this gift from me. For to see your face is like seeing the face of God, now that you have received me favorably" (v 10).

Jacob understood that forgiveness—true forgiveness—is divine. It's something of God, a blessing of grace. Jacob considered Esau's forgiveness to be so miraculous and beautiful that looking upon his brother's face reminded him of the face of God.

"YOU SHOULD FORGIVE YOUR DAD"
One of the first things people told me when I started opening up about what had happened to me was, "You should forgive your dad."

At the time, I was in the ground-zero phase of recovery.

My parents' marriage was imploding; my dad's reputation was in shambles, I was shell-shocked, and gossip swirled all around us.

Adding to my emotional overload was a plethora of confusing messages from Christians. I was told that if I didn't forgive my abuser, Jesus wouldn't forgive me; that you have to forgive even when you're emotionally wrecked; that you can tell someone they're forgiven even while you're still angry; and that forgiveness is something you do for yourself rather than for your abuser.

Some of those are just plain wrong. Some are misleading or blended with truth. So, let's unpack what forgiveness means in the Bible and the empowering message that it is, particularly for survivors.

DEFINING FORGIVENESS

If you look up "forgiveness" in the dictionary, you'll see two basic definitions:

1. *To cease feeling anger or resentment against an offender.*
2. *To give up claim to requital or compensation; to grant freedom from consequences or relief from payment of debt.*

But when it comes to dealing with abuse, particularly chronic or ongoing abuse, we need to be extremely careful how we define forgiveness. On the one hand, letting go of anger is a major milestone in almost every survivor's recovery. On the other, if a battered wife believes she must keep "forgiving" her violent husband, giving up claim to requital and granting freedom from consequences, she may be placed in extreme danger. How we define forgiveness can be a matter of life and death.

I've found it helpful to define two modes of forgiveness: Boundaried Forgiveness and Reconciled Forgiveness.

Boundaried Forgiveness is when we let go of our anger, resentment, and desire for revenge; yet we may maintain boundaries and pursue justice. We do not bear a grudge, but we may file a police report or get a restraining order. The storm inside is quelled, but we won't tolerate further abuse. Boundaried Forgiveness is healthy when our abuser is unrepentant, is in some way damaging to us, or poses an ongoing physical or emotional threat. We aspire to let go of our anger but not our common sense.

In this sense, I've forgiven my dad.

Reconciled Forgiveness is only the ideal when our abuser is genuinely repentant. Their behavior has changed, and we've had time to objectively observe this with a clear head and a mending heart. They've given us space to grieve, they're working on making amends, and we no longer feel threatened or endangered by them. While our relationship may not be perfect or completely restored, a process toward reconciliation has begun.

In this sense, I have not forgiven my dad.

HOW GOD FORGIVES

"Forgiveness" is one of those words tossed around so commonly that everyone assumes that they know what it means. However, it's used in a myriad of different ways, even within the church. Misunderstandings lead us down unhelpful and sometimes dangerous paths, both in terms of our relationship with God and our relationships with others. But if we want to practice Christlike forgiveness, we must first understand the forgiveness of God.

The whole purpose of God's Son becoming human, living a perfect life, taking the punishment for our sin, and rising from the dead was so we could repent, be forgiven, and enjoy reconciliation with God, now and for eternity. Though God's forgiveness is offered to us freely, it's perfectly just, and he paid a terrible price to make it possible: "In [Jesus] we have redemption through his blood, the forgiveness of sins, in accordance with the riches of God's grace" (Ephesians 1 v 7).

1. God's Forgiveness Is Freely Offered—But Not Granted—to All
God is compassionate; he's ready and willing to forgive anyone for anything. He offers his forgiveness to everyone. However, he doesn't grant forgiveness to those who don't want to be forgiven. In Luke 13 v 34, Jesus laments over unrepentant people, saying, "How often I have longed to gather [you] together, as a hen gathers her chicks under her wings, and you were not willing." Though Jesus desires to save and protect, he does not force his forgiveness upon anyone, and many do not want it.

For God so loved the world that he gave his one and only Son, that whoever believes in him shall not perish but have eternal life. For God did not send his Son into the world to condemn the world, but to save the world through him. (John 3 v 16-17)

Don't miss where John writes, "whoever believes in him." God's love and mercy are big and powerful enough to save every soul throughout time and space. Unfortunately, some people are not sorry for their sin, will never be sorry, and have no desire to be forgiven, let alone repent. God's forgiveness is available to them, but they are unrepentant, and so remain unforgiven.

Just so, in our human relationships, we may desire reconciliation with an abuser who isn't sorry. Or perhaps they apologize but have no intention of changing or making things right. They may desire to influence our feelings. They may crave our attention or think we owe them allegiance. However, they don't want biblical forgiveness if they aren't willing to humble themselves, apologize, and change.

2. God's Forgiveness Is Granted on Condition of Repentance

There's a big difference between offering forgiveness and granting forgiveness. God has his own set of boundaries. Unrepentant people aren't allowed in his heaven. He withholds his forgiveness from those who believe they've done nothing wrong and refuse to apologize.

Jesus' very first words in the Gospel of Mark are, "The time has come. The kingdom of God has come near. Repent and believe the good news!" (Mark 1 v 15). Repentance means to turn around completely—to recognize you're wrong, apologize, and change to do what is right. Where there is no repentance, there is no forgiveness. But where there is repentance, God's forgiveness is lavished.

Jesus is God, and God knows everything, including when someone's apology is insincere. He does not grant forgiveness to hypocrites who claim to repent yet have no intention of changing.

In Hosea 6, God's people appear to repent and express faith in God, saying:

> Come, let us return to the LORD …
>> He will come to us like the winter rains,
>> like the spring rains that water the earth. (v 1, 3)

But God sees dishonesty in their hearts and confronts them with their hypocrisy, saying:

> Your love is like the morning mist,
>> like the early dew that disappears.

Therefore I cut you in pieces with my prophets,
  I killed you with the words of my mouth—
  then my judgments go forth like the sun.
For I desire mercy, not sacrifice,
  and acknowledgment of God rather than burnt
  offerings. (v 4-6)

Obviously, we're not all-knowing like God. We mere mortals must be very careful in this area. It's hard to discern between genuine repentance and what is merely manipulation or regret over getting caught. After all, "Sorry" is not particularly hard to say, and "Forgive me" is even easier. It's tempting to trust a liar we love, just as it's scary to trust a repentant person who's hurt us.

Here are a few red flags to watch for. If someone stubbornly persists in sin despite being confronted with it, they are unrepentant. Change is a required ingredient in repentance. People who demand your forgiveness are not repentant either. They are proud. By contrast, when Jacob apologized to Esau, he didn't expect forgiveness, and he didn't merely speak words. Rather, he humbled himself to the ground, wept, and gave Esau lavish gifts. Although genuinely repentant, Jacob did not expect forgiveness or consider himself entitled to it. He approached Esau with much trepidation, sorrow, and shame. A repentant person who understands the gravity of what they've done will never demand forgiveness. In fact, they won't expect forgiveness at all.

3. Once Granted, God's Forgiveness Results in Reconciliation
Once we repent and accept God's forgiveness, he keeps no record of wrongs. In fact, his Spirit empowers us to honor and obey him. He reconciles us to himself, wiping our sins from his sight completely.

*They shall be my people, and I will be their God. I
will give them one heart and one way, that they may
fear me forever, for their own good and the good of
their children after them. I will make with them an
everlasting covenant, that I will not turn away from
doing good to them. And I will put the fear of me in
their hearts, that they may not turn from me. I will
rejoice in doing them good, and I will plant them in
this land in faithfulness, with all my heart and all
my soul. (Jeremiah 32 v 38-41, ESV)*

Forgiveness changes everything. It's our welcome into God's
family. The Judge of the world becomes our Father. "Therefore, there is now no condemnation for those who are in
Christ Jesus" (Romans 8 v 1). For Christians, it's not just
that we went to trial and were found not guilty. It's even
better. It's that we went to trial, Jesus was found guilty in
our place, and we're now completely exonerated, never to be
accused or tried again.

4. God's Forgiveness Doesn't Necessarily Negate Consequences
While my sin can never negate God's faithful forgiveness, it
can result in earthly consequences. If I hurt the ones I love
but repent, God will forgive me. However, those relationships may never recover in this life. If I lie, cheat, or steal,
but repent God will forgive me. However, I may face criminal charges and lose the trust of friends.

In Luke 23 v 32-43, as Jesus hung dying on the cross, he
was flanked by two criminals. One mocked Jesus, saying,
"Aren't you the Messiah? Save yourself! Save us!" But the
other, a thief, rebuked him, saying:

*Don't you fear God ... ? We are punished justly, for
we are getting what our deeds deserve. But this man*

has done nothing wrong ... Jesus, remember me when
you come into your kingdom. (v 40-42)

Jesus answered him:

Truly I tell you, today you will be with me in
paradise. (v 43)

But despite his repentance and Jesus' assurance of pardon,
that thief on the cross still died that day. After Jesus breathed
his last, he lingered on in agony for hours, yet we know he is
now reconciled with God. He was forgiven, but he still had
to endure the earthly consequences of his sin.

WHAT FORGIVENESS IS NOT

Forgiveness doesn't mean giving up boundaries. Forgiveness
doesn't mean amends shouldn't be made, or that behavioral
change can't be demanded. Remember the gifts Jacob offered
to Esau. Remember how the thief on the cross accepted his
harrowing earthly consequences. Remember Jesus, and how
dearly it cost him to make amends on behalf of the sinners
he loves, even though he was without sin.

Forgiveness doesn't mean reconciliation is mandatory. It
doesn't mean there can't or shouldn't be consequences. God
is always patient, but he still follows through with covenant
blessings and penalties. Heaven is described as a city with
strong walls—borders impassable to God's enemies. God
does not allow the unrepentant in his presence, and abusers
need not be permitted in ours.

Beware people who demand forgiveness. Beware those
who pressure you into reconciliation. Unfortunately, a church
leadership team might say, "You need to forgive your youth
pastor, and you should not report him, because when we forgive, we put sin behind us." A parent might say, "If you don't

forgive me, Jesus won't forgive you, and you're supposed to honor me." A spouse might say, "God hates divorce and wants you to be reconciled with me." All such demands betray a lack of understanding of what God says forgiveness is.

A genuinely repentant person will be humble and horrified by their sin. They won't think they are entitled to your forgiveness. They'll give you room to grieve. They'll accept consequences and respect boundaries.

THE LORD'S PRAYER: WHAT DID JESUS MEAN?
When Jesus taught his disciples to pray, he famously said they should say:

> *Our Father in heaven,*
> *hallowed be your name,*
> *your kingdom come,*
> *your will be done,*
>   *on earth as it is in heaven.*
> *Give us today our daily bread.*
> *And forgive us our debts,*
>   *as we also have forgiven our debtors.*
> *And lead us not into temptation,*
>   *but deliver us from the evil one. (Matthew 6 v 9-13)*

Then he concluded:

> *For if you forgive other people when they sin against*
> *you, your heavenly Father will also forgive you. But if*
> *you do not forgive others their sins, your Father will*
> *not forgive your sins. (v 14-15)*

"If you do not forgive others their sins, your Father will not forgive your sins." Doesn't this contradict everything I've been saying?

First, we must never impose works theology—the view that I need to do something in order to earn God's favor—onto the Savior of grace. That is because we know from Jesus' own words that we don't earn God's love by being super-good:

> *It is not the healthy who need a doctor, but the sick.*
> *I have not come to call the righteous, but sinners.*
> *(Mark 2 v 17)*

Nothing we do, including our forgiveness of others, can earn God's blessing, nor will it ever be perfect. God's not counting up your acts of forgiveness until there are enough to buy his love, nor is he waiting for believers to fail so he can withdraw his salvation. As a Christian, I cannot lose the love of a faithful God. So, what does Jesus mean?

Don't overlook the fact that Jesus' prayer presupposes repentance. He was talking to believers, who had asked God, "Forgive us our debts." Many times, Jesus defined his good news as "repentance for the forgiveness of sins" (Luke 24 v 47). We acknowledge our sin, turn to Jesus, and ask for forgiveness. Just so, we seek to forgive those who acknowledge their sins and turn to us for forgiveness.

When we repent and Jesus forgives our sins, we're empowered by his Spirit to forgive others when they too genuinely repent. If we cannot forgive others, even when they're sorry, either the Spirit is still working forgiveness in our heart, or we need to throw ourselves on his mercy and ask him to gift us his perfect healing peace.

We emulate Jesus because we love Jesus, not because we must be as good as Jesus to be loved by him. Like adoring children, we repeat things we hear our Father say, and do what we see him do. I seek to forgive, carefully and biblically, because I desperately want to honor my Father. I'm not trying to earn my place in his family. I know I can't! I don't fear God reneging on his love because I'm not quite as awesome as he originally thought (after all, he knew all my sins, failures, and weaknesses long before I was even born). My forgiving others is not a work that earns my salvation, but a grateful response to God's forgiveness of me.

FORGIVE, BUT MAYBE LATER

Whether we realize it or not, forgiveness is what we ultimately desire. As a survivor, when I was eventually enabled to forgive my dad, my agonizing (albeit justifiable) anger abated. Even righteous anger, I've learned, is exhausting and distressing. I felt like I'd been running an emotional marathon for decades, and I was finally able to rest and have peace.

Remember Boundaried Forgiveness and Reconciled Forgiveness. If being reconciled with an abuser is dangerous or too painful, Boundaried Forgiveness may give you relief. However, if even Boundaried Forgiveness feels impossible, we can breathe easy, taking our time to heal. We can place our trust in Jesus as the Giver of peace and grace and ask him to work forgiveness in our hearts in time. God isn't holding a stop-watch over our recovery process. We should aspire to forgive eventually, but we don't stand unforgiven by God until we reach that point of forgiving others. God is ready and willing to heal, no matter how broken, devastated, and angry we may feel. We can cling to God, as Jacob did, and ask him to bless us.

Serious wrongs necessitate serious proof of change. Painful emotions can't be swapped out for happy ones like lightbulbs. Abusive behavior isn't something to sweep under a rug, and Jesus would never endorse doing so. God wouldn't have us lie by pretending we're all better when we're justifiably upset. Jesus doesn't ask us to trust dangerous people or tolerate sin. Anytime we're counseled—either by an abuser or someone else—to "forgive" in the sense of forgetting, ignoring, or accepting abuse, we can be certain their counsel is not of God.

As survivors, we're used to unrealistic expectations. Trained to acquiesce and undervalue ourselves, we feel a heightened awareness of rules and judgment. We felt our abuser's disdain with every fiber of our being. As a result, when forgiveness is demanded by those who seem good and wise, we tend hurriedly to conform, because we're desperate for acceptance.

When churches and counselors teach forgiveness as a work that earns our salvation or proves we're real Christians, they set the wounded up for failure. What should have been our hope of future peace and rest is warped into an impossible standard that we're left to achieve alone and a legalistic nightmare that we're left to navigate alone.

We want to prove we're good people. We want to demonstrate our strength, recovery, and virtue by forcing super-human behavior. Just as when we were victims struggling to appease our abuser, now we're survivors anxious to prove to God, our church, or even ourselves, that we're not as broken as we feel.

But eventually we realize we don't feel forgiving. We feel raw. We crave justice. We're still disturbed and distrustful. We fear our abusers could still harm, deceive, or manipulate us. We feel like hypocrites for faking happiness, and foolish for daring to hope. Like Sisyphus, of Greek mythology, we feel condemned to repeatedly roll a boulder uphill only to have it roll back down, for eternity. What we intended for good has backfired, heaping shame on our pain.

Oftentimes, it's an abuser who guilts us into forgiving them. Maybe they claim they're sorry, and tell us that if we're a good person, we'll trust their sincerity. Maybe they demand forgiveness and feel entitled to reconciliation. They accuse us of being unloving, coldhearted, or emotionally abusive if we distrust them. They can't forgive us for not forgiving them, so they accuse us of being unforgiving, just like them.

Exhausted, we tell our abuser that we forgive them. We tell ourselves that we've forgiven them. Then when our wounds, which were in the process of knitting together, are ripped open by a careless word, broken promise, or a rough patch in our ongoing cycle of grief, we feel stupid, weak, and defective. We feel that our efforts to recover have failed, and we're plunged into the depths of shame and grief. At this point, it's long past time to seriously consider the damage that premature or misdefined forgiveness is doing to us.

1. Premature forgiveness denies survivors time to process emotions
To play off a popular passage from the book of Ecclesiastes, there is a time to forgive and a time to be wary; a time to be reconciled and a time to set boundaries; a time to grieve and a time to heal. Though our abusers may still be alive, we've experienced a loss in the sense that our relationship, hopes, and dreams of how life could be have died. Just like someone who's suffered the death of a loved one, we experience stages of grief. These include anger, denial, and depression.

Allowing ourselves to feel angry—to process that emotion and express it honestly—is a vital part of the recovery process. While it may seem endless, overwhelming, and even dangerous, confronting our anger and dealing with our pain is the only way to grow beyond it. Too often we're pressured to prematurely forgive, skipping this vital step. However, our anger is an expression of how much we loved our abuser. If we had not loved them, and had not desired their redemption, we would not be so upset.

Our anger is proof that we're aware of God's law: that we know that God is righteous and injustice is offensive. Our anger is a sign that we long for a better world: one where there is no sin, tears, or pain.

2. Premature forgiveness puts the responsibility of reconciliation on the victim, instead of the perpetrator
During my teens I took a CPR class. One of the things they taught was to take frequent breaks. If you're trying to resuscitate someone, but you faint from exhaustion, you're not helping that person but complicating the crisis. Likewise, if you see someone drowning, you're to call for help and throw them a life preserver. Jumping into the water is a last resort, because the drowning person could pull you under in their panic.

Just so, if we're emotionally exhausted and spiritually compromised, we need to take a break from trying to spiritually resuscitate our abuser. If they're unrepentant, drowning themselves in sin, we must maintain a safe distance to avoid being pulled into their damage. As my CPR teacher advised, we need to get help. Throw them a life preserver, such as a pastor or police officer. Trust others to confront them with their sin and breathe grace into their soul. Ultimately, the only one who can save your abuser is God. It's not your responsibility to fix them.

Some of the wisest counsel I ever had, oddly enough, was from a computer hacker, who said, "You're a Christian, but you're not Jesus Christ. He died so you wouldn't have to be crucified. Don't suffer their abuse because you think that by doing so, somehow you can save them. You're just enabling their sin when you let them treat you like that."

3. Premature forgiveness enables abusers
In the case of emotional or spiritual abuse, abusers chip away at our happiness and confidence one sliver at a time until

we're easy to break down and control. Because of this, it's risky to remain in contact with an abuser, especially during the ground-zero stages of recovery. Covert manipulation and mind games fly easily under our radar. Our abuser knows our weak spots, vulnerabilities, and insecurities, because they put them there. They know just where the injuries are to rub salt in—all the while feigning innocence—because they made them. They hold the keys to our heart.

Some will suggest creating "boundaries" in order to control how much influence an abuser has over us. This is feasible once you've graduated to a moderately recovered state. However, what some fail to realize is that all it takes to inject pain into our minds is a disdainful glance, carefully crafted insult, or cleverly planned manipulation. By definition, an abuser has failed to respect boundaries before, so we cannot trust them to respect boundaries now. It takes a lot of work, heightened awareness, and assertiveness to enforce boundaries, which may be too daunting and exhausting for a grieving survivor to attempt.

In Acts 15 v 36-41, Paul expresses deep distrust of his ministry partner Mark, because Mark deserted him during a previous missionary trip. Paul refuses to travel with Mark at all, and it takes several years for Paul to forgive Mark and view him as a "fellow worker" (Philemon v 24). By the end of Paul's life, around 20 years later, he'd come to view Mark as a useful ministry partner (2 Timothy 4 v 11).

Survivor, you can tell your abuser that you need time and space to heal before you can forgive them. You can tell your pastor that you aren't emotionally objective enough to handle any relationship with your abuser. You can tell your counselor that even boundaries would compromise your peace of mind. You can say that, because your trust was betrayed over the course of so many years, it may take you that many years before you're ready to be reconciled.

Premature forgiveness to a broken heart is like a band-aid on a stab wound. You cannot tell someone, "I forgive you," while you're emotionally and spiritually hemorrhaging. Wait for the bleeding to subside or stop. Forgive when you are ready. Forgive after your abuser has lost their power to manipulate and re-open your wounds. Forgive yourself for not being able to save your abuser. Relinquish that earnest desire to fix, help, and control. Find a safe distance, remove yourself from the influence of evil, and breathe.

WHAT MAKES FORGIVENESS POSSIBLE?

There are two basic errors we need to avoid when it comes to forgiving abusive people. First, we want to avoid mistaking forgiveness for pretending you're OK when you're not. Second, no matter how much we're hurting we need to avoid losing hope, thinking that forgiveness is impossible, or unnecessary. Though it may feel like we're endlessly bleeding pain, the God of peace can heal our hearts and our minds.

Forgive yourself if you still feel anger and sorrow years after a traumatic experience. If you can't talk to your abuser without anxiety, you don't have to talk to them. If you can't look at your abuser without anger, you don't have to look at them. If you can't read a birthday card from your abuser without suffering a depressive slump, you can tear the card up and throw it away unopened.

You don't owe them more of your time, let alone more of your suffering.

Don't rush forgiveness. Don't force forgiveness. Don't forgive before you're ready. Don't feel ashamed if you find yourself spiraling down after you really thought you'd recovered. Don't beat yourself up if you genuinely forgive and they betray you yet again. Their sins are not your sins. Fixing them, or not, is God's job, not yours.

Even if our abuser is unrepentant, by grace we may eventually find peace in Boundaried Forgiveness. Paul tells us, in Romans 12:

> *If possible, so far as it depends on you, live peaceably with all. Beloved, never avenge yourselves, but leave it to the wrath of God, for it is written, "Vengeance is mine, I will repay, says the Lord." (v 18-19, ESV)*

We can rest in the knowledge that God is just. We can release our anger, praying:

> *I can no longer carry this pain inside me. Jesus, just as you suffered for sin in my stead, I trust you now to be angry in my stead too. Be the righteous judge you are, because everything you do is good. You will punish evildoers. I trust you to be the arbiter of justice, so I can rest and find peace.*

While Reconciled Forgiveness is dependent upon our abuser's repentance and change, our peace and contentment need not be. As Paul implies, it's not always possible to "live peaceably with all." There comes a time when we've done all we can but reconciliation isn't a goal shared by our abuser. In times like these, when pain overwhelms and peace feels unimaginable, pray to Jesus and rest in his power to heal.

Instead of rushing what can't be rushed, focus on building your relationship with God. Meditate on his word. Cling to your Savior. Pray he fills you with his Spirit, working faith and forgiveness in you. For what is forgiveness if not love, joy, peace, patience, kindness, goodness, faithfulness, gentleness, and self-control? These are not feelings we can demand or virtues we can fake. These are the fruit of the Spirit. So, rest now and cease your striving. Enjoy God's grace. Entrust your recovery to the Savior, who gave his life to recover you. You may find that in good time, the forgiveness you've longed for or even bitterly resisted washes into your soul like rain after a drought.

13. DEFINING LOVE

Dear children, let us not love with words or speech but with actions and in truth.

(1 John 3 v 18)

Survivors often find it difficult to form healthy relationships, especially romantic ones. Our blueprint for love and marriage may be based partly or wholly on our parents' broken model, and our expectations may be warped and misaligned by interactions with a violent boyfriend or manipulative wife. We tend to either stick with what we're familiar with or leap as far away from it as possible. Both reactions can be disastrous.

Whether we subconsciously cling to what we know or rebel against it, this behavioral pattern can be observed in almost all people, survivor or no. Someone who grows up mainly eating fast food may struggle to eat healthily as an adult. The child of entrepreneurs will likely be hardworking and ambitious. Someone raised in a family of athletes will likely be athletic or marry an athlete, or swing in the opposite direction to a lifestyle where sports and fitness are taboo. Although ultimately we're responsible for our own actions and attitudes, being aware of the influence that our past has can mean the difference between wise strategic choices and unhelpful instinctual reactions.

Sexual-abuse survivors may find themselves repeatedly reliving their rape in a string of one-night stands and hyper-sexualized relationships. A man who was abused by his father and undefended by his mother may find himself distrustful of and angry at women, while a man abused by his mother may partner with girlfriends who berate him, replicating his childhood verbal abuse. A woman abused as a girl may attract a string of brutal drunks or sexual predators, or swing to the opposite extreme of fearing men, seeking shallow and passive relationships. An emotional-abuse survivor may find herself pushing away female friends in hopes someone will care enough to hold on, while being excessively vulnerable with men, hoping just one will consider her valuable enough to protect her from himself.

Sadly, we must confront the possibility that we don't truly understand what love is. Our recipe for love may include ingredients like manipulation, control, paranoia, sexual deviance, and even violence. We may find, to our great sorrow, that we don't know how to feel loved by someone who doesn't hurt or degrade us. And we may find, to our horror, that we don't know how to express love or communicate emotion in a way our loved ones understand.

So, let's rewind a bit.

What is love versus what we're looking for? What are our needs versus our wants, and what's healthy versus what we're used to? How do we differentiate authentic love from sexual obsession, narcissism, or an egotistical desire to control?

1 Corinthians 13 v 4-7 maps it out beautifully for us. Keep in mind, these verses are exemplified only by Jesus himself. No fallen human can fulfill these, yet as children of God we desire to imitate his standard. In a healthy relationship, each person will attempt to model Christ's love to the other. Thus, by studying the list in these verses, phrase by phrase, we can aspire to an ideal of godly love, both in

our search for love from others and in our endeavor to love others well.

LOVE IS PATIENT

Thomas could not believe that Jesus had risen from the dead. Despite the testimony of his friends and fellow disciples, he lamented, "Unless I see the nail marks in his hands and put my finger where the nails were, and put my hand into his side, I will not believe" (John 20 v 25). Despite having known Jesus for years, witnessed his miracles, and even seen Jesus raise others from the dead, Thomas was incapable of believing he was alive again.

How did Jesus respond to Thomas? Did he irritatedly snip, *After everything I've done to show you that I'm God, how can you doubt me?* No. Rather, he appeared to Thomas, took him by the hand, and patiently worked through his doubts with him, saying, "Put your finger here; see my hands. Reach out your hand and put it in my side. Stop doubting and believe" (v 27). Jesus, the most trustworthy person in the universe, wasn't offended by Thomas's distrust. He was patient with Thomas and lovingly attended to his doubts and fears.

A patient person won't rush you into major life decisions, and that includes matters involving trust and reconciliation. They won't write you off when you get things wrong. Rather, they'll spend time with you, gently helping you and listening to your troubles with a desire to understand. They'll walk with you through your pain and fear.

LOVE IS KIND

In Mark 10, parents brought children to Jesus so he could bless them. Imagine those kids: crying babies, squirming toddlers, and snotty-nosed preschoolers with messy hair and bruised knees. The disciples tried to shoo the tired parents and raucous young ones away, but Jesus said, "Let the little children come to me, and do not hinder them, for the kingdom of God belongs to such as these" (v 14). Then Jesus laid his hands on the children and prayed for them (though it's safe to wager he had to catch a few of them first).

A loving person is kind. They want what's best for you, and they don't embarrass you or make you feel unwanted. They desire to take care of you, even when it's inconvenient, climbing into the trenches of your life. They avoid situations that might make you uncomfortable or put you at risk. They're there for you during challenging times. They never give you reason to fear them, but make you feel wanted and needed.

LOVE DOES NOT ENVY

Once, a rich young ruler came to Jesus and asked, "Good teacher ... what must I do to inherit eternal life?" (Mark 10 v 17; Luke 18 v 18). Knowing he wanted to earn his own way into heaven, Jesus answered:

No one is good—except God alone. You know the commandments: "You shall not murder, you shall not commit adultery, you shall not steal, you shall not give false testimony, you shall not defraud, honor your father and mother." (Mark 10 v 19)

The ruler replied to Jesus, "I've done all these things." But Jesus said:

One thing you lack ... Go, sell everything you have and give to the poor, and you will have treasure in heaven. (v 21)

At this, the man was downcast and he left, for he was extremely wealthy (v 22). Jesus' response was that...

it is easier for a camel to go through the eye of a needle than for someone who is rich to enter the kingdom of God ... With man this is impossible, but not with God; all things are possible with God.

(v 25, 27)

Most people would envy this ruler's youth, political influence, and affluence. Most people would have told him what he wanted to hear to ingratiate themselves or earn brownie points. Jesus did not. Instead, he pitied him. This man was clinging to earthly wealth and losing sight of spiritual wealth. He wanted to earn God's acceptance, or buy his ticket to heaven, but prized the things of this world over the things of God. By relying on his own merit rather than Christ's mercy, he placed himself beneath a terminally crushing load.

Jesus didn't envy others or covet their lot in life. Contrariwise, he dedicated himself to completing his divine mission: the redemption of those whom he loves. Just so, we're to mutually share the mindset of Jesus as we sacrificially love and humbly serve one another (Philippians 2 v 5). We aspire to do nothing out of egotism or self-importance, but rather to act in humility, putting each other first. Before his birth, in the wonderfulness of heaven, God's Son did not consider divine glory something to be grasped but gave up his glory to become human, to live and die as one of us—even the lowliest among us.

A person cannot envy you and also genuinely love you. When we envy others, we love what they have more than we love them. Someone who loves you won't selfishly isolate you, damaging your relationships to keep you for themselves. They won't resent your promotion at work, healthy friendships, or other blessings. Their attitude toward you will be one of mercy and benevolence. Just as Jesus desired the rich young ruler's salvation, so a loving person will desire your wellbeing.

Granted, someone who loves you may still get jealous. For example, if a wife spends more time with friends than with her husband, he may have a legitimate complaint. If a husband cheats on his wife, it would be strange and concerning if she didn't feel jealous. Perhaps it's helpful to distinguish between legitimate jealousy, and envy—where envy is coveting what God has chosen to give someone else, and jealousy is wanting to get back what God has rightfully given you. So, while a loving person may grow jealous, they will not envy, and neither jealousy nor envy are defining qualities of their personality.

LOVE DOES NOT BOAST
In Mark 8, Jesus and his disciples were traveling between villages when he asked, "Who do people say I am?"

> They replied, "Some say John the Baptist; others say Elijah; and still others, one of the prophets."
> "But what about you?" he asked. "Who do you say I am?"
> Peter answered, "You are the Messiah."
> Jesus warned them not to tell anyone about him.
> (v 28-30)

For all his miracles, sermons, and holiness, Jesus had no desire to be a rock star. The Lord of the universe didn't come to demand service. His priority was never his own praise. He wasn't self-important, vain, or entitled. Ironically, he associated with commoners, prostitutes, the poor, and the broken. He was humble, laying aside his glory to focus on others—to show them grace and to build them up. Just so, when we love others, we don't rub our merit in their faces. We put aside our pride and love humbly.

LOVE IS NOT PROUD OR ARROGANT

Just before Passover, in the middle of dinner, Jesus stood up and left the table. He knew the Father had given all things into his hands, and, laying aside his outer garments, he took a towel and tied it around his waist. He poured water in a basin, got down on his knees, and went around the table washing his disciples' feet. He then dried them using the towel around his waist (John 13 v 3-5).

Keep in mind, the disciples weren't rich or fashionable men. They were fishermen and travelers who walked dirt roads and never had a pedicure. Jesus was demonstrating, in picture form, how shocking it was that the Lord of glory would wash away the sins of his friends. When Jesus came to Peter, Peter asked, in effect, *Lord, how can someone as wonderful as you wash my feet?* Jesus answered, "Unless I wash you, you have no part with me" (v 8).

Jesus was humble. He was graciously willing to get down in the dirt of other people's lives. Not only did he graciously confront them with their sin, but he went to the cross to wash their sin away. He humbled himself and cleansed his people.

Just so, a loving person will be merciful and humble toward others. They aren't too proud to help and serve. They'll authentically apologize and graciously offer to forgive. If the relationship is healthy, they'll partner with you to help you overcome sins you're struggling with. They won't brandish your problems against you, yet they'll respect you enough to be honest with you. They'll value your wellbeing more than how you affect them. That means they'll tell the truth humbly in love, even if you might get angry at them for saying it. When a loving husband takes on a leadership role in his marriage, he'll do so in such a way that his wife knows they're a team: that he appreciates, respects, defers to, and hears her.

LOVE IS NOT RUDE, IT DOES NOT DISHONOR OTHERS

In Luke 7 v 36-50, Jesus attends a community dinner in the home of Simon the Pharisee. The Pharisees were popular religious scholars—considered experts in the law, they took obedience to God very seriously. As they were eating, a woman notorious for her sins wandered amid the gathering. Bringing a costly flask of ointment, she dropped to her knees beside Jesus, weeping, kissing his feet, and wiping them with her long hair.

Simon was mortified. *If this man were truly a prophet,* he thought, *he wouldn't let this impure woman touch him.*

But Jesus answered Simon's thoughts with a story.

> *Two people owed money to a certain moneylender. One owed him five hundred denarii, and the other fifty. Neither of them had the money to pay him back, so he forgave the debts of both. Now which of them will love him more?"*

> *Simon replied, "I suppose the one who had the bigger debt forgiven."*

> *"You have judged correctly," Jesus said.*

> *Then he turned toward the woman and said to Simon, "Do you see this woman? I came into your house. You did not give me any water for my feet, but she wet my feet with her tears and wiped them with her hair. You did not give me a kiss, but this woman, from the time I entered, has not stopped kissing my feet. You did not put oil on my head, but she has poured perfume on my feet. Therefore, I tell you, her many sins have been forgiven—as her great love has shown. But whoever has been forgiven little loves little."*

*Then Jesus said to her, "Your sins are forgiven …
Your faith has saved you; go in peace." (v 41-48, 50)*

Jesus refused to play politics. Instead of flattering the prestigious and influential Pharisee, he did the last thing most
would have expected: he honored the social reject, the outcast, the damaged, and the abandoned. Judging the woman's
repentance to be authentic, he forgave her sins and wel-
comed her friendship and love, defying cultural norms and
religious legalism.

A loving person will treat others honorably, defending the
weak against judgment and dishonor.

LOVE DOES NOT INSIST ON ITS OWN WAY

In Luke 22 v 39-46, Jesus visited the Garden of Gethsemane
to pray with his disciples. Knowing his crucifixion was imminent, he fell on his knees, wept, and prayed, "Father, if
you are willing, take this cup from me; yet not my will, but
yours be done" (Luke 22 v 42).

A loving person understands that sometimes—oftentimes—what's right is also what's difficult. Love is loyal,
willing to make sacrifices in order to strengthen a relationship or spare others pain. Someone who loves will combine
a humble desire to serve with devotion and self-denial. Jesus
knew his death would be agonizing and humiliating, yet he
submitted to his Father's will as the only way to save the
people he loves.

LOVE IS NOT IRRITABLE OR EASILY ANGERED

John the Baptist was languishing in prison, likely expecting to die there. The prophet of God who heralded the
coming of the Messiah, who baptized Jesus in the Jordan,
and professed faith in Jesus as the Christ, was apparently
faltering in faith. He sent his disciples to ask Jesus, "Are

you the promised Savior, or should we look for another?"
And Jesus answered:

> *Go back and report to John what you hear and see:*
> *The blind receive sight, the lame walk, those who*
> *have leprosy are cleansed, the deaf hear, the dead are*
> *raised, and the good news is proclaimed to the poor.*
> *Blessed is anyone who does not stumble on account of*
> *me. (Matthew 11 v 4-6)*

Unlike Jesus, as sinful people we often have a false sense
of entitlement. We feel we deserve praise, and to have our
wants anticipated, our needs served, and our efforts accepted with gratitude and adulation. When we don't get these
things, we tend to get irritable or angry. Ironically, Jesus
didn't act entitled. Despite being the holy, glorious, only
begotten Son of God, he didn't mind reassuring the weak
and comforting the doubtful. He was not irritable or easily
angered. He was patient, gentle, merciful, and kind.

A loving person works to keep their temper in check.
They don't seek to win an argument just for the sake of
winning. They don't drive home their point with a clenched
fist or vindictive insult. And they'll strive (though, being
human, likely not succeed completely) to not be snappy, irritable, or ornery.

LOVE KEEPS NO RECORD OF WRONGS

In Mark 2 v 1-12 we read about four men who decided to
bring their paralyzed friend to Jesus for healing. When they
couldn't reach Jesus because of the crowds, they lugged the
man up to the top of the house, tore a hole in the roof, and
lowered his bed into the room where Jesus preached. Marvel-
ing at their faith, Jesus said to the paralytic, "Son, your sins
are forgiven" (v 5). He then healed his physical disability too.

The man rose up, picked up his bed, and went home.

When we express faith in Jesus, he is faithful. He doesn't rub our noses in past offenses. He doesn't act on the basis of our past but on his own perfect love. By his grace, we can rise up out of the paralyzing effects of sin, pick up our cross, and follow Jesus home to heaven.

Just so, in our inter-human relationships we aspire to avoid grudges. Unlike an abuser, we desire a quality of love that doesn't exhume old sins long repented of. We don't humiliate our loved ones over amended failures, or use each other's pain as ammo. This doesn't necessarily mean we trust, but that we seek blessing and justice rather than revenge.

LOVE DOES NOT DELIGHT IN EVIL OR REJOICE AT WRONGDOING

In John 2 v 13-17, Jesus traveled to the temple in Jerusalem. When he saw salesmen selling cattle and money-changers advertising, he was overcome with zeal for God. Making a whip from cords, he beat them all out of the temple, sent their coins crashing, and overturned their tables. So great was his love for pure worship that he yelled, "Stop turning my Father's house into a market!" (v 16).

Jesus took no delight in knowing his people were being taken advantage of. He was not impressed by slick opportunists profiting from the commercialization of worship. He reacted in righteous anger out of love for God and love for God's people. Just so, a person who loves you will never rejoice in your deception or oppression. Rather, they will defend you from it, wherever they find it, no matter how influential or outwardly religious the perpetrators may be.

LOVE REJOICES WITH THE TRUTH

Upon witnessing God work miracles through many of his disciples, Jesus said, "Rejoice that your names are written in heaven" (Luke 10 v 20). He too rejoiced, saying, "I praise you, Father, Lord of heaven and earth, because you have hidden these things from the wise and learned, and revealed them to little children" (v 21).

Someone who loves you will rejoice to see your faith growing, your hope strengthening, and your character being built up in Christ. They won't pressure you to sin, laugh at your weakness, or revel in your failures. Like Jesus, they'll rejoice to see God working in you and through you.

LOVE ALWAYS PROTECTS

Early one morning, John recounts in his Gospel, Jesus arrived at the temple to teach. The teachers and specialists in the law brought a woman before him. Hoping to catch Jesus teaching false doctrine, they challenged him, saying,

> *This woman was caught in the act of adultery. In the Law Moses commanded us to stone such women. Now what do you say? (John 8 v 4-5)*

After they had pestered him, Jesus finally responded, "Let any one of you who is without sin be the first to throw a stone at her" (v 7). When they heard this, they could not contradict him, and wandered away, dumbfounded. Then Jesus stood up and asked the woman, "Where are they? Has no one condemned you?" She replied, "No one, sir." And Jesus said,

> *Then neither do I condemn you. Go now and leave your life of sin. (v 11)*

A loving person will defend us against oppressive and cruel people, as well as works-theology devoid of grace. They'll treat us mercifully and forgive us for sinning, but also entreat us to sin no more. They'll "desire mercy, not sacrifice," (Matthew 12 v 7), and while they cannot pay for our sins the way Jesus did, if we wander from the truth of the gospel, they'll seek to bring us back and so save our souls (James 5 v 19-20). They'll seek to protect us from temptation, the sin of others, and false accusations.

LOVE ALWAYS TRUSTS

Let's travel back to the Garden of Gethsemane. As Jesus prayed, he was wracked with anxiety, knowing his torture and death were imminent. So great was his agony and fear, his sweat became as drops of blood falling to the ground (Luke 22 v 44). "Father, if you are willing," he prayed, "take this cup from me; yet not my will, but yours be done" (v 42).

Jesus trusted the plan of God. He knew that humanity was dead in sin. He knew they needed a Substitute to take their place in the courtroom of heaven. He trusted his Father and Spirit to raise him from the dead, so he would be victorious over Satan and the grave. However, that didn't make Jesus' suffering any less painful, nor his apprehension any less terrible. His trust took him along a hard path. He trusted himself to his Father, and his followers to his Father.

When we love someone, we trust God to save them. We don't try to control them, manipulate them into submission, or guilt-trip them into conformance. Sometimes, loving an abusive person means stepping out of their lives, praying, "God, not my will, but yours be done."

LOVE ALWAYS HOPES

1 Peter 1 v 3-5 tells us that because of God's great mercy, he causes his children to be born again to a "living hope." Thanks to the resurrection of Jesus Christ from the dead, we're heirs with him of an inheritance that is imperishable,

undefiled, and unfading, which is prepared and kept in heaven for all those who by God's power are guarded and preserved through faith for eternity.

Like God, someone who loves us will desire the building up of our faith and the establishment of our hope and peace. They'll yearn for a better future, guard our hearts, and rejoice in the grace and mercy of Christ, our hope.

LOVE ENDURES ALL THINGS, LOVE ALWAYS PERSEVERES

In the Garden of Gethsemane, as Jesus sweated blood and prayed, a mob was approaching. They were led by Judas, his former disciple and friend. As Judas leaned in to embrace his teacher…

> *Jesus asked him, "Judas, are you betraying the Son of Man with a kiss?"*
> *When Jesus' followers saw what was going to happen, they said, "Lord, should we strike with our swords?"*
> *And one of them struck the servant of the high priest, cutting off his right ear.*
> *But Jesus answered, "No more of this!" And he touched the man's ear and healed him.*
> *Then Jesus said to the chief priests, the officers of the temple guard, and the elders, who had come for him, "Am I leading a rebellion, that you have come with swords and clubs? Every day I was with you in the temple courts … But this is your hour—when darkness reigns." (Luke 22 v 48-53)*

Love exists in two states. There is love as an emotion—the warm, compassionate, belonging feeling we all crave. But there is also love as an action—when we do what is best for someone, even though it's difficult and unpleasant.

Jesus emotionally loves the children of God. He comforted the woman caught in adultery, reassured Thomas when he could not believe, and astounded Peter with his humility. However, he also showed love as an action to his enemies: to Judas who betrayed him, to the high priest's servant, and to all those falsely accusing him. In love, he challenged their sin, healed the man's ear—demonstrating his divinity to them—and called them to repent even though he knew many of them would not.

Emotionally, I do not love my dad. When I search my heart for feelings for my father, I find only disgust and the gaping scar where my adoration used to be. While it may sound strange, letting go of that emotional love was a massive healing milestone for me. It wasn't until I stopped loving my abuser that I was finally able to forgive him. As the last ember of my love was extinguished, my anger over not being loved by him died too. Emotional love was replaced with forgiveness. Anger was replaced with peace.

Loving an abuser can be like trying to love cancer. Every experience is painful. Sometimes, it's even life-threatening. If we give them our heart, they break it. If we trust, they betray.

For years I prayed for my abuser, but eventually I had to stop. The very thought of him injected so much anxiety into my prayer life that prayer itself became something I dreaded. If I prayed for him before bed, I was plagued by insomnia and nightmares. So, I asked Jesus if he could pray instead: if he could pray for my abuser on my behalf. Jesus carried my sins to the cross. Now he carries my crushed hopes to God.

But I didn't lose emotional love. Rather, I reoriented it. I transferred my love of my biological father entirely and permanently to my heavenly Father. He alone is faithful. He alone will not break me. Yet while my emotional love for my abuser is gone, I can still love as an action. I can report his crimes and hope he never hurts anyone else. I can set boundaries and refuse to enable his sin. I can call him out when he's cruel, selfish, or perverse, and hope he repents. Why? Because I love God.

If there's any remote chance that my abuser is (or will become) a child of God, then out of love for my heavenly Father, I'll do what's right. In a very real sense, that is showing love to my abuser, even though my abuser may not appreciate it, and I only feel revulsion for him.

Jesus' love endures in such a miraculous, amazing, divine way that he can love the worst of sinners, soften their hearts, and draw them to repent. As mere human beings, we cannot do that. Not only am I unable to save, but I am so far beneath Jesus in my ability to love that my love "endures" only in the sense that I'm clinging to the hem of Jesus' robes and he's dragging me along behind him.

My love endures in the sense that I protect my kids from my abuser. I've separated myself entirely from those who damage my faith and emotional wellbeing. I guard my heart from people who would harass or belittle me, so I can be the best mom, wife, and daughter of God I can be (Proverbs 4 v 23). Like Jacob, after he wrestled with God, I grasp the ankle of the Lord and beg him to bless me with peace. When human relationships fail and emotional love runs cold, our love perseveres in the form of actions, and our love for our Savior endures by his grace.

YOU WILL FAIL. BUT GOD!

No mere human can live out 1 Corinthians 13 v 4-7 perfectly. No one can love like Jesus. That's why he came! Yet, by God's grace, when we fail, we'll recognize our sin, repent, and aspire to change. Remember, the difference between an abuser and a Gracer lies in their reaction to their actions. It's how we respond to our failures to love well which demonstrates whether we truly love or not. Some abusers might prove they don't love by continuing to abuse despite correction. Others might prove that they are beginning to grow toward true love by protecting us from themselves. This may mean they go to rehab, seek counseling, create boundaries for themselves, give us space to recover, or step out of our lives completely.

Some abusers exist in a state of constant darkness: apathy, selfishness, perversion, or violence. Others exhibit cycles of faux-improvement, mimicking repentance and change only to backslide into sin and dysfunction again. Those who continually seesaw between evil and fake goodness can be particularly deceptive and heartbreaking, making our reliance on God all the more vital.

A person who loves you may fail in every manner of ways. I know I've failed Jason many times. But a loving person will listen to loving correction, knowing that though it can be hard to hear, it is necessary for character to be built. Also, a loving person will forgive when you're sincerely sorry. Pain and shame will not amuse or enrage them. Rather, it will inspire regret and sympathy. This is never an easy process, but it's an important part of spiritual growth and healthy relationships. A recognition of faults and an authentic attempt to change are signs that we're growing in a positive direction.

Too often we settle for the kind of love we think we deserve: a counterfeit love resembling our abuser's lies. However, love isn't about getting what you deserve. Love is a gift, a choice, and a promise. Love is a determination. To love is to declare war on your selfish desires and overcome darkness with mercy and grace. It won't always be a warm, fuzzy feeling. Often, it's a lot of work. It's trudging through another person's pain and helping them recover. It's humbly apologizing when we make mistakes. Love is protecting another from pain yet being humble enough to tell them a painful truth. Love loves the person more than the relationship, and love may sacrifice that relationship in order to save the person from themselves. Love is a constantly growing, ever changing, organic determination to be good and do good like Christ.

Love like that is only fully embodied and exemplified in one person: Jesus. If I demand it in all its perfection from a fellow sinner, I'll be disappointed and they'll be crushed. Nevertheless, I can look for seeds and traces of it, and celebrate it when I see it in others. I can learn to be loved by those who love me, and to love those who love me.

I'm still learning what love is. I don't expect to ever completely understand it this side of heaven, but I do plan to live my life in constant study of Christ, the God-Man, so I may learn to love better and to treasure the love I find in others. I was raised in a home where "love" was control, fear, and secret-keeping. "Love" was the tolerance of evil and the silence of the suffering. It wasn't until I married a loving man that I realized how apathetic my father was. It wasn't until I had children of my own that I saw how unloving my own childhood had been. It wasn't until I grasped a small snippet of God's love that I began to understand the truth. Because of my relationship with the Lord who calls himself Love, I can toss those old dysfunctional blueprints aside and replace them line by line with the blueprint of Jesus.

This is how we know what love is: Jesus Christ laid down his life for us. (1 John 3 v 16a)

14. THEN I AM STRONG

If I can stop one heart from breaking,
I shall not live in vain;
If I can ease one life the aching,
Or cool one pain,
Or help one fainting robin
Unto his nest again,
I shall not live in vain. (Emily Dickinson)

"I feel like I can talk to you," he said to me one day. "I feel like we have something in common—a darkness."

At first, I wasn't sure what my friend meant. Evil? Surely not. Depression? Possibly. But then I realized he was talking about pain. It's a perfect word for it, I think.

When Jason and I went on our honeymoon, we toured Cave of the Winds in Colorado. At one point, in a deep beautiful cavern, the guide switched off the lights. What I saw then was the deepest blackness I've ever experienced. You couldn't see your hand an inch from your face. And while there were probably 20 people in the cavern with us, unless they spoke you could not tell they were there at all.

The kind of pain my friend was talking about is like darkness. It's something like sadness blended with fear mixed with regret and a twinge of despair. It's the thing we find overwhelming: the thing we can't communicate or explain, and maybe do not want to. Like the blackness of that cavern, this emotional, spiritual pain is vast, deep, unbounded, and all-encompassing. It's the thing that makes us feel alone. The thing we fumble blindly through and can't navigate. The thing that frightens us with its bleakness. The thing we can't see the end of.

Yet, as the prophet Isaiah once said, "The people walking in darkness have seen a great light; on those living in the land of deep darkness a light has dawned" (9 v 2). I have seen that Light break through my darkness. The brighter it shines in my life, the farther the shadows fall behind me.

OVERCOME EVIL WITH GOOD

Joseph was the son of Jacob, and his epic tale takes up almost all of Genesis 37 – 50. While his life began in comfort, he came to know the darkness of pain. He was his father's favorite son. He had ten older brothers, who grew murderously jealous of Joseph as their father doted on him and gave him a beautiful coat. Adding to their frustration, God blessed Joseph with prophetic dreams foretelling that one day his brothers would bow down to him (Genesis 37 v 1-11).

So, one day, in the pasture, the jealous brothers attacked their teenage brother. They tore the beautiful coat off him and threw him into a pit, where they kept him hostage. When human traffickers passed by, the brothers sold Joseph into slavery, and he was taken away to Egypt, a leading nation of the day. Later, the brothers showed their father Joseph's ripped coat, which they'd dipped in the blood of a slaughtered goat, and claimed he'd been slain by a wild animal (v 12-36)).

Meanwhile, Joseph was bought as a slave by a prestigious Egyptian officer named Potiphar. God was with Joseph, and Potiphar admired Joseph's work—but Potiphar's wife admired Joseph's appearance. As I mentioned in an earlier chapter, she tried to seduce him. Day after day she asked him to sleep with her, but he refused to betray his master or sin against his God. When Potiphar's wife threw herself at Joseph, he ran from her, so she falsely accused him of rape out of spite (Genesis 39).

But God was with Joseph, even then. After being cast into prison, word of Joseph's God-given ability to interpret dreams spread, until Pharaoh himself called on him for advice. Realizing Joseph was supernaturally blessed, Pharaoh freed him from prison and set him in a place of high authority (Genesis 41).

Forty years later, Joseph again encountered his treacherous brothers. By then, he looked completely different. He'd escaped the shackles of slavery, had been exonerated, was recognized as a wise and godly man, and had found favor as prime minister over all of Egypt. When famine swept the land, people from far and wide came to Joseph for food. His brothers were among the crowd, but they didn't recognize the brother they'd betrayed.

When Joseph revealed his identity, understandably they were terrified and said, "Behold, we are your slaves." But Joseph was not set on vengeance. He replied:

You intended to harm me, but God intended it for good to accomplish what is now being done, the saving of many lives. (Genesis 50 v 20)

Joseph had found purpose in his pain. He realized that—though his past was fraught with trials and injustice—thousands were now being saved from starvation, including the people of God, because God had had a plan all along. Joseph's traumatic journey had led him to a position of power through which he could bless others and advance God's will. I imagine this comforted him, and played a large role in his recovery as well as in his forgiveness of his repentant brothers.

Joseph's story is dramatic and miraculous, and while ours may look different than his, we too can find comfort by finding purpose in our pain. Perhaps our suffering empowers us to empathize with others. Maybe it inspires us to volunteer for charity, or offer unique insight to pastors and church leaders. Maybe it makes us better and more protective moms and dads. Maybe it draws us to place our faith in Christ, or roots us in that faith more deeply.

Whatever the case, realizing that God will work a purpose for our pain—that it's not arbitrary or pointless chaos—makes our pain less like darkness. Just as God created light in the black nothingness before creation, he can create light in the dark cavern of our broken hearts. No longer is our suffering futile, meaningless, or useless. It has a purpose. It has great power.

In Romans 8 v 28, Paul echoes Joseph and applies this concept to all who love God, saying, "We know in all things God works for the good of those who love him, who have been called according to his purpose." That means that no matter how dark things get, no matter how distant I wander or how far I fall, God will remain faithful, and will use my pain for something beautiful.

No matter how powerful abusive people or even Satan himself may seem, we can know that God is sovereign. This doesn't mean that he's the creator, instigator, or cause of evil, but it does mean that he's far more powerful than any evildoer. He is in control. Not a single hair can fall from our heads without his knowledge. We may not know exactly why—or all the reasons why—God lets bad things happen. We may never understand this side of heaven. Nevertheless, we can be confident, knowing that he is good and he is faithful, and that we can put our experiences to good and healing use.

What an abuser intended for evil, God can use for good. In my life, he has already begun! Like gathering fragments of broken glass, he collects my shattered peace and wounded heart to design a mosaic of his redemptive love.

Just think, if God had never empowered me to survive abuse, or guided me through the Valley of the Shadow of Death, I might not have lived past the age of 15. I might never have understood his incredible love and powerful mercy to the depth that I do. I might never have realized that he is faithful even when I am not, and he is present even when I feel abandoned and alone. I might not have learned to live by faith and not by sight. I might never have found my husband or become a mother determined to be careful and kind. Yes, I was harmed, but God is bigger than my abuser, and he has used my experiences for good.

THIS THORN IN THE FLESH

When I told a dear friend that, after I'd reported my dad's abuse to police, a relative had compared me to Potiphar's wife, my friend replied, "Oh no, Jennifer, you're like Paul." I was a bit taken aback. As a woman, I tend to identify most strongly with women in the Bible. It had never occurred to me—and frankly it felt audacious—to imagine having much in common with a pivotal apostle and writer of Scripture like Paul. But what my friend meant was that Paul understood pain. In fact, Paul's philosophy on how to view suffering and overcome hardship has been intrinsic to my recovery.

In 2 Corinthians 12 v 7-10, he says:

I was given a thorn in my flesh, a messenger of Satan, to torment me. Three times I pleaded with the Lord to take it away from me. But he said to me, "My grace is sufficient for you, for my power is made perfect in weakness." Therefore, I will boast all the more gladly about my weaknesses, so that Christ's

*power may rest on me. That is why, for Christ's sake,
I delight in weaknesses, in insults, in hardships, in
persecutions, in difficulties. For when I am weak,
then I am strong.*

We don't know the nature of Paul's thorn, and I don't know the nature of yours. But I do know the nature of mine. I begged God to take away what I was living through—to change my dad, fix my family, and repair the damage to my relationships. Like Paul, God answered my prayers by enabling me to endure and survive, but not by taking away my pain. His grace—his love, mercy, and salvation—are exemplified powerfully in my life, because when I was weak, he was strong.

Was it my own optimism or positive thinking that spared me from suicide? Did I, as a foolish teenage girl, somehow discern truth from lies in a life overpowered by mind-games and hypocrisy? Was it, when I was 21, my own good judgement and maturity that saw me marry a godly man who would protect me? No. Of course not. I fumbled my way through the darkness of pain and the chaos of abuse, clinging to a thread of God's grace.

I won't lie to you: there were many times when I could not feel God. In fact, as a child and teen, I didn't expect to live to adulthood. I thought my dad was righteous as far as men went, and that all men were as dangerous as he was or worse than him. I believed I'd eventually give up and put an end to my misery. So, whether I anticipated being raped and murdered or committing suicide, I never dreamed of married life, or picking out baby names, or having a career. Making it to college, I thought, was a long shot.

My soul felt desolate. My heart grew cold. My mind was overwhelmed by sorrow and fear. I was incapable of wise decisions and powerless to muster my own faith or hope. I didn't believe I could ever be happy. But God had wrapped that thread of grace around me. And here we are, on the brink of the future.

YOU ARE NOT YOUR PAIN

I'm sure that, as Joseph sat at the bottom of that pit, or was marched down the road in a slave-trader's caravan, or languished in prison falsely accused of rape, he felt shattered and distraught. But forty years later, he did not identify as a victim. Rather, he identified as someone who could rely on God to keep his promises. He identified as someone whom God was working in and working through to save lives.

Despite his ongoing "thorn in the flesh," Paul did not view himself as a victim either. Remarkably, even though he had been oppressed, imprisoned, beaten, and slandered, he viewed himself as someone privileged to be loved by God, and whose hardship was being used by God to comfort, encourage, and build others up in faith.

What an extraordinary attitude! And what a beautiful philosophy for us as survivors to adopt. Because, you see, our pain doesn't have to define us. We don't have to identify as victims, or addicts, or damaged, or use whatever other labels we may give ourselves. While labels may help diagnose our problems, they can have a side-effect of boxing us in. When they come to define us, they can also confine us.

I used to think of myself as a victim. And I was. But I learned that when I viewed myself as a victim, so did other people. Abusers, predators, and manipulators can sense pain. They seek out the weak, the suffering, and the vulnerable. I attracted perverse and controlling individuals to such an unsettling extent that I began calling myself a "freak magnet."

Acknowledging myself as a victim, and seeing my abuser for what he was, were pivotal first steps in breaking free from abuse. But I couldn't remain in that state forever. Pitching your tent in a mindset of perpetual victimhood stunts recovery. It's like having an open wound that won't stop bleeding. You've got to acknowledge the wound, yes. But then you have to work out how to bind it up.

So, you see, the labels we give ourselves are incredibly important. They can mean the difference between living indefinitely in victimhood, or recovering by the grace of the ultimate Survivor, Jesus Christ. They can keep us paralyzed in outrage, insecurity, and hopelessness, or motivate us to push past our obstacles and achieve a better way of life. A life where we can see beyond the darkness of sin and look forward to life with our true Father, in heaven.

Never forget who you are. Never forget who you can become. You are so much more than a label, a statistic, or part of a demographic. You are not your past. You are not your victimization. You are not evidence in a police report or a few lines in a newspaper article. You are not your paycheck, your sexuality, your job, your accomplishments, or the car you drive. You are someone who is created in the image of God. You are intrinsically valuable and wonderfully made. And if you place your faith in Jesus, you are a child of God himself.

As Paul says in Galatians 3 v 28, "There is neither Jew nor Gentile, neither slave nor free, nor is there male and female, for you are all one in Christ Jesus." God does not identify his children based on their ethnicity, nationality, social standing, or gender. He doesn't pretend those things don't exist, but he sees all those who love Jesus first and foremost as his beloved children—as his kids. We find our identity—our unity and our wholeness—in Jesus. I have found that when I stop focusing on my pain, guilt, shame, and sin, and start focusing instead on Christ—as counterintuitive as it may sound—my agony loses power over me. He's the light at the end of the tunnel. His glory chases my shadows away.

God made you for a reason. You are not a random accident in need of finding meaning or a purpose. You already have a purpose. You are exactly who you're meant to be, where you're meant to be, when you're meant to be, right now. Let God work in you to heal and mature you, and you'll grow more and more into the person he ultimately designed you to be. As humans, our perspective on life is limited. We are like ants walking on the surface of a huge painting, trying to understand what it is, but too close and small to see the big picture. Just so, we only see a tiny fraction of our life-story at once, but that doesn't mean it isn't beautiful or intelligently designed.

In Jason's favorite movie, *The Count of Monte Cristo*, the hero tells his protégé:

> *Life is a storm, my young friend. You will bask in the sunlight one moment, be shattered on the rocks the next. What makes you a man is what you do when that storm comes.*

He is right. Life is often hard. But as a Christian I have a Savior who calms the winds and the waves. I have a Redeemer who has weathered earthly suffering. He is my anchor through the storms of this world. He is my Creator who made me, my Shepherd who guides me, and my Father in heaven, waiting with open arms to welcome me home.

And those last four sentences you just read are equally true of anyone and everyone who puts their faith in Jesus.

Don't be afraid if you feel lost. We all feel lost from time to time. Joseph did. Paul did. Jesus himself was racked with anxiety as he wept and sweated blood in the Garden of Gethsemane. But you were custom-made by the Lord of the universe himself. That is a privilege unequaled and immeasurable. He has a plan for you. He has a purpose for your life. He can use your experiences—both good and evil—to work beauty and hope in a dark world.

If you ever need to find yourself, all you have to do is find your Creator. I've learned that the search for myself is futile if I ignore the God who has made me for his purpose and his meaning. Like the vessel on a potter's wheel, we sometimes feel like life is spinning too fast, forcing us into uncomfortable shapes. But that doesn't mean we aren't works of art. It simply means we're works of art in progress.

Like Joseph, we can now say of our abusers, "They intended to harm me, but God intended it for good to accomplish what is now being done." In my case, God used my pain to accomplish, in part, what is now being read. If this book helps one person heal—if it can stop one heart from breaking, ease one life of its aching, or soothe one pain—I consider my suffering a worthwhile endurance. As Paul said, "When I am weak, then I am strong." God's grace is sufficient to carry me through any adversity, and it shines brightest in the darkness. By the grace of Jesus, and for the sake of Jesus, I am at peace with my past, and rejoice in the hope that it brings hope to others.

Life flows on in endless song
Above earth's lamentation
I hear the sweet, though far-off hymn
That hails a new creation
Through all the tumult and the strife
I hear the music ringing
It finds an echo in my soul
How can I keep from singing?

What though my joys and comforts die?
The Lord my Savior liveth
What though the darkness gather round?
Songs in the night he giveth
No storm can shake my inmost calm
While to that refuge clinging
Since Christ is Lord of heaven and earth
How can I keep from singing?

I lift my eyes; the cloud grows thin
I see the blue above it
And day by day this pathway smooths
Since first I learned to love it
The peace of Christ makes fresh my heart
A fountain ever springing
All things are mine since I am his
How can I keep from singing?

When evil looms and darkness falls
And tragedy is breaking
When all that's good seems overturned
By God I'm not forsaken
For though I fall or wander far
I'm not too far for saving
And when my Shepherd seeks and finds
How can I keep from singing?
                    (Verses 1-3, Public Domain;
            Final verse, Jennifer M. Greenberg)

ACKNOWLEDGMENTS

For Jason: I began this book as a series of letters to help you understand me better, and somehow came to understand myself better in the process. I set out to find myself, and found more of Jesus along the way. Thank you for faithfully showing me how our Savior loves.

For my daughters: Someday you'll be old enough to read this book and understand why some loved ones are missing from our lives. I'm so sorry for that, and I love you more than life, my baby girls.

For Carl Laferton: One of my biggest fears was the editing process, but you have been far kinder and taught me more than I ever thought possible, transforming what I feared into a blessing. Thank you for being my editor, counselor, and friend. You gave me my voice.

Special thanks to Joe Henegan, James Burstow, and everyone at The Good Book Company for telling my story and being an example of God's grace in my life; Russell Moore, Daniel Darling, Phillip Bethancourt, and everyone at ERLC; Christina Bostick and ICON Media Group; my incredible endorsers, advocates, and friends too numerous to name; and Dr. David Murray, Pastor J.D. Greear, Rachel

Miller, Pastor Todd Bordow and Cornerstone OPC, Pastor Robert Arendale, Allen and Sharon Greenberg, Jason and Amber Arcemont, Doug and Joelyn Laughlin, Candace Runaas, Erin Rothchild, Bryan Kirk, Tony Gonzales (you're still my bouncer), and Megan Lively, for your endless encouragement and wise counsel. I thank Jesus Christ for you all.

Thank you to the many abuse survivors who selflessly shared your stories with me during the writing and editing process. Your honesty, trust, and prayers gave me the insight, motivation, and grace I needed to finish *Not Forsaken*. This is our story.

And finally, thank you, God, for getting me through things I can hardly believe I survived. When I look back on my life, I see your salvation.

thegoodbook
COMPANY

BIBLICAL | RELEVANT | ACCESSIBLE

At The Good Book Company, we are dedicated to helping Christians and local churches grow. We believe that God's growth process always starts with hearing clearly what he has said to us through his timeless word—the Bible.

Ever since we opened our doors in 1991, we have been striving to produce Bible-based resources that bring glory to God. We have grown to become an international provider of user-friendly resources to the Christian community, with believers of all backgrounds and denominations using our books, Bible studies, devotionals, evangelistic resources, and DVD-based courses.

We want to equip ordinary Christians to live for Christ day by day, and churches to grow in their knowledge of God, their love for one another, and the effectiveness of their outreach.

Call us for a discussion of your needs or visit one of our local websites for more information on the resources and services we provide.

Your friends at The Good Book Company

thegoodbook.com | thegoodbook.co.uk
thegoodbook.com.au | thegoodbook.co.nz
thegoodbook.co.in